KEN PYE
MERSEYSIDE TALES

KEN PYE
MERSEYSIDE TALES

CURIOUS & AMAZING TRUE STORIES

FROM HISTORY

First published 2015

The History Press
The Mill, Brimscombe Port
Stroud, Gloucestershire, GL5 2QG
www.thehistorypress.co.uk

Reprinted 2016, 2017

British Library Cataloguing in Publication Data.
A catalogue record for this book is available from the British Library.

ISBN 978 0 7509 6293 3

Typesetting and origination by The History Press
Printed in Great Britain by TJ International Ltd.

CONTENTS

Acknowledgements

It would not have been possible to produce such a broad collection of stories without help and support. I would therefore like to thank the staff of Liverpool Central Libraries and of the Liverpool Record Office in particular; and the librarians, and many of my fellow proprietors, of the Liverpool Athenaeum. I am, as always, very grateful for their encouragement, time and professionalism.

Introduction

I am a Scouser born and bred, and I am deeply proud of this. I love the city and its people, and the remarkable history and heritage that make these so special. Liverpool in particular, but also so much of the rest of Merseyside, has played a major role in the economic, industrial, commercial and cultural growth and life of Britain – and the world. This is why studying and learning about its past is endlessly rewarding.

However, as well as all the important people and significant events that have shaped us, the story of our region is one of fun and fascination. This is especially so when we delve into the more curious stories of the place and of its many eccentric and noteworthy individuals – hence this book.

This is an entirely miscellaneous collection of what I think are some of the best tales in the region and those that will amuse, surprise and entertain my readers; in fact, I am sure that there is something for everyone in this assortment. All of my stories are true (although some are more true than others), and they all prove that, indeed, 'truth is stranger than fiction'.

I certainly hope that you enjoy reading these *Merseyside Tales* just as much as I enjoyed researching and writing them.

So, let's begin with a tale about Cowboys and Indians, and how they came to Liverpool, twice, and how they were brought here by one of America's most popular folk heroes and greatest showmen, Buffalo Bill Cody.

Ken Pye
Liverpool, 2015

Merseyside Tales

The Wild West Comes to Liverpool

In 1847 the great American Wild West legend Buffalo Bill was born in Iowa, USA. His real name was William Frederick Cody and, when little more than a boy, he became a rider for the pioneer mail delivery service the Pony Express. In 1861 he began working for the US Army as an Indian scout and he fought in the American Civil War from 1861 to 1865.

Cody earned his more familiar nickname when he became a hunter for the Kansas Pacific Railway in 1876, tracking, shooting and killing North American bison, more commonly known as buffalo. This was to

Buffalo Bill's Wild West Show programme cover.
(*Discover Liverpool Library*)

supply fresh meat for the workers building the great railway that was connecting the east and west coasts of the fledgling country. Bill was an expert shot with a rifle and very skilled at his trade; so much so that he was said to have killed 4,280 buffalo in eighteen months, and his record was forty-eight of the great animals killed in just fifty minutes.

The problem was that he, and the riflemen he had working for him, almost completely wiped out the species and drove the Plains Indians into starvation as a result. This was one of the causes of the Indian Wars in which Cody fought, gaining popular fame as a 'Wild West Hero' for single-handedly killing Yellowhand, the Cheyenne chief.

Cody became renowned across America and then around the world as the great 'Buffalo Bill' and, in 1884, he began to capitalise on his fame by creating a travelling Wild West Show. He toured the world with this spectacular entertainment, taking it to the greatest cities of the world and, of course, one of the greatest at the end of the nineteenth century was Liverpool. He first brought his show to the 'crossroads of the British Empire' from 6–18 July 1891, where it was performed twice daily in Newsham Park – and what a show it was!

The men and women of this great extravaganza, with their animals and equipment, arrived at Knotty Ash station on Sunday 5th aboard a single train of seventy-two carriages. These were carrying 200 performers, including cowboys, rough-riders and Native American Indians. There were also 200 horses, dozens of covered pioneer wagons and a herd of buffalo! They made their way through the suburbs of Liverpool to the park, attracting vast crowds of astonished onlookers en route.

Thousands of people came from across Merseyside every day, paying 1s a time to see the show. In the huge outdoor arena they witnessed the roping and branding of cattle, the horsemanship skills of the rough-riders and the recreation of a Sioux Indian attack on a wagon train. This featured the real-life Native American Indian chiefs Short Bull, Kicking Bear and Long Wolf.

Scousers had never seen anything like this before and gasped in awe at the authentic sights, sounds and smells of the men and animals, and of the gunshots, flames and smoke. They cheered in exhilaration at the nick-of-time rescue of the Pioneers by the American Cavalry in all their uniformed glory. Extra ferries had been laid on to carry spectators across the river, and extra trams and omnibuses brought people from across the city and beyond to shout in thrilled excitement as the one-and-only, authentic, actual Deadwood Stage Coach was attacked by bandits.

Adults and children alike were amazed to see the world-famous sharp-shooter Annie Oakley (known as Little Sure Shot) shoot the pip out of an Ace of Spades at 100yds distance! But to see the great man Buffalo Bill himself ride into the arena, leap down from his horse and sweep off his hat in a spectacular bow really brought the crowds to their feet.

Here he was in person, just as they had seen him in photographs in the newspapers and in sketches in the 'penny dreadful' comics they had all been reading. With his long, flowing white hair, curling moustache and neatly trimmed goatee beard, and in his white buckskins, fabulous boots with engraved buffalo figures, and wearing his silver six-guns with their pearl handles, Buffalo Bill brought the Wild West to life in Liverpool.

At the end of the two-week run, a quarter of a million people had seen the show and £20,000 had been taken in ticket sales – £2 million in today's money. Bill was so happy with his profits that, in May 1903, he came back to visit us again. This time, however, he stayed for three weeks after arriving in three trains of carriages. He brought with him over 500 horses, but there was no Annie Oakley. Even so, there were now even more Indians, from the Sioux and Cheyenne nations. There were over 100 rough-riders and, as well as a contingent of US Artillery and Cavalry, a detachment of English Cavalry 'flew the flag' for the British Empire in a show of militaristic alliance with our ex-colonial cousins from across the Atlantic Ocean.

This time the Wild West Show took place in a massive, purpose-built Exhibition Arena on Edge Lane Drive. This stood where the Corporation Bus Sheds were later built and where the extension to the Technology Park now stands. It was 185ft wide by 440ft long and had tiers of seats on three sides. Outside, and covering an additional 10 acres, was an accompanying exhibition of displays and attractions, including a recreated Indian Village. The most popular character in the show this time round though, apart from Buffalo Bill himself, was the Lakota Sioux Indian chief, from the Black Hills of South Dakota, Charging Thunder.

My nan saw the show this time round and she told me how, as a young girl, she was on Wavertree Road when Buffalo Bill, in his Buckskins, boots and gunbelt, went shopping, accompanied by Charging Thunder. The tall, somber Indian chief was dressed in a plain grey smock and leggings, with equally plain moccasins, and was wearing two feathers in the back of his hair. He seemed to be absolutely delighted with the shopping bags he was carrying, one in each hand, but which were both filled with nothing but cabbages. He was proudly showing these to the fascinated crowds lining the pavement, declaring to them as he did so, 'Cabbages, Cabbages!' Meanwhile, Bill was bidding the gawping shoppers a 'Howdy Pardners!' and a 'Glad, ta see ya'll!', as locals no doubt responded with such comments as 'Orlright der Bill la!' and 'Giz a go ovya guns Billy mate!'

Chief Charging Thunder's life, however, was to change forever when the Wild West Show left Liverpool and moved on to Salford. Here, the 26-year-old Native American Indian chief decided to leave the show with one of Buffalo Bill's horse handlers, a girl named Josephine. They married and moved first to Darwen but finally settled in Gorton, Manchester, where they set up home and raised a family.

Changing his name to George Edward Williams, he worked for many years at Belle Vue Circus where he looked after the elephants; his favourite of these was named Nelly! George and Josephine lived a happy married life until the former Lakota Sioux Chief caught pneumonia and, on 28 July 1929, sadly died at the age of only 52. He lies buried in Gorton cemetery as George Williams, with Josephine, who died in 1943, but their descendants still live in and around Manchester.

Buffalo Bill Cody himself, despite his worldwide fame and all the money he made, became bankrupt in 1915. He died in poverty in 1917, at the age of 70. His body lay in state in Denver, Colorado, for just a day, but 25,000 people filed past his coffin to pay silent tribute to the great Indian scout and showman.

The memory of his two visits to Liverpool, with his amazing and spectacular Wild West Show, lived long in the hearts and minds of Liverpool people, and we shall certainly never see the like of Buffalo Bill again!

THE WIDNES AND RUNCORN TRANSPORTER BRIDGE

Sometime in the ninth century, the daughter of Alfred the Great, Queen Ethelfleda of the Mercians (*c.* 870–918), built a castle on the shore at Runcorn, overlooking the river across to what is now the town of Widnes. From the reign of King John (1167–1216) a small ferryboat was rowed across the Mersey from Runcorn Gap to Widnes West Bank. The tolls levied for this went directly to the Crown, but if a traveller could not afford the boat ride then at low tide he could take his life into his hands and cross the river on foot, but he still had to pay a much smaller toll to the lord of the manor for the privilege of doing so!

The Widnes to Runcorn Transporter Bridge as it looked in 1939.
(*Courtesy of Liverpool Athenaeum Library*)

The ferry service operated almost continuously for centuries and a report on it written in 1835 stated:

> The public are ferried across by a couple of men, who are not always to be found at a moment's warning; next, the landing-place at Runcorn is at all times extremely incommodious; and thirdly, that on the other side is still worse; in fact, at low water, the passenger here steps out of the boat on a plank, lands on mud and sand, and after walking on this compost upwards of a hundred yards to the ferry-house, he has then a mile to proceed at all events.

In 1864, work began on the London and North Western Railway Company's impressive Runcorn Bridge. This still carries main-line trains in and out of Liverpool and is officially named the 'Queen Ethelfleda Viaduct'. This is because when it was being built workmen discovered the foundations of the Saxon queen's ancient castle, which had been demolished many years before.

However, the ferry still rowed its way across the river but only until 1887 when work began to dig the Manchester Ship Canal. This runs alongside the Wirral bank of the Mersey and is separated from the river by a wall. After the canal had been completed the ferry trip had to then be made in two parts. One boat rowed across the river and another rowed across the canal, and passengers had to climb over the canal wall to complete their journeys!

As well as this, an increasing number of vehicles, of all kinds, were now wanting to cross between Runcorn and Widnes and so a road bridge was clearly now required at this point on the river. To meet this need, in 1899, the Widnes and Runcorn Bridge Company was formed.

However, it would be very expensive to construct a bridge that could carry coaches and carts across the river and be at a height to allow ocean-going ships to pass beneath it. An alternative was needed, so the company decided that a 'transporter bridge' would solve their problem.

A 'transporter' consisted of two tall iron towers, one standing on each side of the river. These were connected from their highest points by a gantry carrying parallel tracks. A trolley travelled along these, from which, suspended on cables, a large 'carriage' moved from one side of the river to the other. The first transporter bridge in the world had been opened, in 1893, in Bilbao, Spain, and this had been followed, in 1898, by transporter bridges in Rouen in France and in Bizerte, which is now in Tunisia. This meant that the technology was proven and, in 1901, work began on building the Widnes and Runcorn Transporter Bridge.

Work was completed in 1905 at a cost of £130,000 (around £12.5 million today), and the massive towers each stood at a height of 180ft (55m). The gantry spanned a distance of 1,000ft (300m), which made this the largest transporter ever built. The carriage, which was more like a giant tea-tray, weighed 250 tons and was 55ft (17m) long and 24ft 6in (7.5m) wide. It had been designed to carry 'four two-horse wagons or 300 passengers', and there was a shelter for the passengers as well as a cabin for the driver. This was mounted at one end of the carriage and was tall enough to give him a clear view in all directions.

The journey across took two and a half minutes, and this amazing contraption was driven by electric motors in the trolley, fed from a power house in the tower on the Widnes side. However, the bottom of the carriage passed only 12ft above the high water level and only

4ft 6in above the wall that separates the Ship Canal from the River Mersey. This meant that trips across had to be timed to allow ships to pass beneath.

For journeys on the Transporter the tolls were 6*d* (6 old pence) for carriages, carts and motor vehicles, and 1*d* (1 old penny) for foot passengers and animals. These were only increased in 1953, when they went up to 1*s* (1 shilling) and 2*d* (2 old pence) respectively. Despite the volume of traffic that used the bridge it never made a profit and was run as a public service by Widnes Corporation, who had bought it in 1911.

In the years immediately following the Second World War the Transporter was carrying an average of 500 cars, 300 lorries and trucks, 100 bicycles and 4,000 foot passengers every day. By the late 1950s these figures had risen to an annual average of 280,000 cars, 145,000 commercial vehicles and over 2 million foot passengers, and I remember travelling on the Transporter as a child. This was on outings with my family, in my father's Ford Prefect saloon car, and mostly to places like Chester Zoo or Delamere Forest. I recall how we shared the journey with great crowds of people as well as vehicles, and sometimes with horses and small herds of cattle or sheep!

But time was running out for the old suspended carriage system and it was becoming overused and overcrowded; it simply could not keep pace with modern transport needs. A fixed, high-level bridge now had to be built, which opened in 1961 and is now named The Silver Jubilee Bridge. The Widnes to Runcorn Transporter Bridge was demolished soon afterwards, and it has now passed into the mists of nostalgia.

DICKIE LEWIS – LIVERPOOL'S GREAT BRONZE NUDE

Directly facing the Adelphi Hotel, at the corner of Ranelagh Street in Liverpool, stands a gracious building that was originally built as 'Lewis's Department Store'. This was the fourth store on the site to bear the name of its founder, London-born David Lewis (1823–1885), the first opening in 1856. But, in 1886, the year after its founder's death, the store was completely destroyed by a disastrous fire. However, this provided the opportunity for the building to be entirely redesigned, developed and rebuilt.

'Liverpool Resurgent' dominating the front entrance of the former Lewis's Department Store. (*Discover Liverpool Library*)

Business was so good that the store was rebuilt and enlarged again, between 1910 and 1923, by the renowned architect Gerald de Courcy Fraser (1872–1952). His design incorporated a roof garden, with tame monkeys and parrots, exclusively for the use of Lewis's wealthier patrons. This was the first large store in Britain to have a fully installed sprinkler fire system, and it was the first shop in Liverpool to use full-size mannequins, or dummies, to display clothes in the shop windows. This gave rise to the local expression for a lazy or dilatory person, 'You're standin' there like one of Lewis's!'

However, in the Second World War, during the May Blitz of 1941, Liverpool was subjected to almost continuous bombardment by the German Luftwaffe. Indeed, the city was the most heavily bombed city in Britain, outside London, in sheer tonnage of Nazi incendiary and high-explosive bombs. Lewis's Ranelagh Street store became one of many architectural and commercial casualties. Nevertheless, the store was completely rebuilt after the war by the same architect. This time, De Courcy Fraser designed it with a steel frame encased by a façade of Portland Stone, and it reopened in 1951.

To appropriately mark the significance of the new store and the continuing resurrection of Liverpool after the war, the sculptor Jacob Epstein (1880–1959) was commissioned to create a special statue for the front of the building. His instructions were to create something large and imposing that would represent the strength and resilience of the port and city of Liverpool. Epstein took his commission seriously and set to work.

Shrouded in mystery as to the final form of his work, it took Epstein two and a half years to complete. It was then mounted above the grand entrance doors but remained hidden under massive tarpaulins so that his design would stay secret. Then, on 20 November 1956, came the official unveiling.

All the 'great and good' of Liverpool were assembled on Ranelagh Place, outside the front of the building, along with the staff and management of Lewis's Store and thousands of eager Liverpudlians. There was an expectant buzz amongst the crowds because word had leaked out that the statue that Epstein had created would be very special indeed. And then the cord was pulled and the great shrouds fell away.

Some loud cheers went up but also great shouts of amazement. Some of these were in shock and outrage, whilst others were exuberant shouts of delight! This was because what had been exposed – quite literally – was the much larger than life-size, blatantly full-frontal figure of a great, naked bronze man.

There he still stands, with a determined expression and stance, on the prow of a great ship that seems to be surging out of the front of the building; he is piloting the vessel forward, going boldly into the future! The bronze ship's prow weighs 2½ tons, and the figure itself weighs a further 2¾ tons. He stands at 18ft 6in high overall, but I have no information about any other dimensions associated with the figure!

Because the statue is cast in perfect and detailed physical accuracy, his sudden appearance in one of Liverpool's busiest thoroughfares, and above one of its most popular department stores, generated many complaints and letters to the local newspaper, the *Liverpool Echo*. After a fortnight the reaction died down, although it was said that for weeks after the unveiling the front bedrooms of the Adelphi Hotel were all booked up and mostly – though not exclusively – by women!

Despite the notoriety surrounding Liverpool's great bronze nude man, I find the attention paid to his manhood somewhat unnecessary; proportionally he is not that impressive – but that is just a personal view! However, whilst the official name of the Lewis's statue is Liverpool Resurgent, it is known locally, and for obvious reasons, as 'Dickie Lewis'!

'Over the Sticks' – The Founding of the Grand National

Towards the end of 1828 a Liverpool hotelier and entrepreneur named William Lynn (1794–1872) decided to expand his business interests with a brand new venture. His idea was to run flat-races for horses, which was then a very popular pastime all over Lancashire, especially amongst the aristocracy and the moneyed classes. It was also a great favourite with the general public, because horse racing is such an exciting spectator sport.

Indeed, flat-races had been running in the Maghull area of north Liverpool from the previous year, but Lynn was convinced that he could organise these more effectively and more profitably. So for financial backing he took his idea to Sir William Philip Molyneux, the 2nd Earl of Sefton (1771–1838). Lord Sefton was also known locally as 'Lord Dashalong' because of his fondness for driving a carriage and four 'at breakneck speeds' around the streets of Liverpool town. This meant that the earl found Lynn's idea appealing, so he agreed to finance him and also to make land available at Aintree, also just to the north of Liverpool.

Lynn immediately enclosed a large area of this land and set out his new racecourse. The foundation stone for the racetrack's first grandstand was laid by Lord Sefton on 7 July 1829, and Lynn ran three flat-races that year alone. These became so successful that by 1835 the Liverpudlian entrepreneur had decided to make his Aintree races even more exciting by changing them into steeplechases. This form of horse race had become increasingly popular because it was much more challenging and competitive than a race over flat ground.

The term 'steeplechase' – colloquially known also as a race 'over the sticks' – actually comes from the very earliest horse races, which took place across open countryside. The horses would literally race from church steeple to church steeple, over a prescribed distance, jumping whatever natural or man-made barriers they found in their way.

So to replicate the hedges, brooks and walls that horses would encounter across open country, Lynn now built a series of fences and obstacles on his racecourse. His first Aintree steeplechase was held in

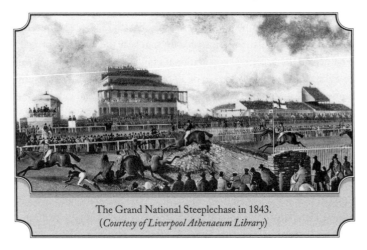

The Grand National Steeplechase in 1843.
(*Courtesy of Liverpool Athenaeum Library*)

1836 and was an immediate triumph. The winner was Captain Martin Becher, riding The Duke, and very soon the race became known as The Grand Liverpool Steeplechase.

Because of his continuing success, Lynn now decided to diversify his sporting events with an entirely different form of animal race. Once again he approached Lord Sefton, who not only agreed to finance this venture too but also to make more of his land available, this time at Altcar, between Liverpool and Ormskirk. Lynn's new idea was for a hare-coursing event, which he named 'The Waterloo Cup' after his popular and luxurious Waterloo Hotel. This once stood on Ranelagh Street, on a site now occupied by the entrance to Liverpool's Central Station.

The new competition involved a hare being released from one side of a large area of land, generally hedged. A few seconds later two or three greyhounds would also be released to see which, if any, would be first to catch and kill the hare. Lynn's first Altcar meeting also took place in 1836 and attracted huge crowds. It was won by a greyhound bitch named Melanie, which was owned by Lord Molyneux, the eldest son of the Earl of Sefton. As well as winning prize money of £16, the aristocrat was awarded a silver snuff box as a trophy. The Waterloo Cup soon became profitable and very popular, always attracting great crowds often numbering in tens of thousands. In modern times, however, the cruelty of hare-coursing attracted attention of a different kind, and the sport was declared illegal in 2005.

By 1839, Lynn's annual Aintree steeplechase had now also become outstandingly popular and profitable. In that year the race was formally renamed as The Liverpool and National Handicap Steeplechase, and on 26 February an estimated crowd of 50,000 spectators saw Lottery romp home as the undoubted winner. It was from then that the race became generally – but not officially – known as 'the Grand National'.

Lottery therefore entered into the record books as the first horse to win the famous Grand National Steeplechase. This animal was a great favourite with the crowd and seemed to enjoy all the attention; however, the horse absolutely hated his jockey, Jem Mason. This meant that the rider had to creep up on the horse from behind and quickly mount him before the animal realised who it was that was climbing onto his back!

A certain Captain Becher was also riding in the 1839 race, on a horse named Conrad, but he fell into a 6ft-wide brook at one of the fences. The captain afterwards said that he 'never knew water tasted so foul without whisky in it'. This jump has been known as 'Becher's Brook' ever since.

This obstacle is just one of the sixteen challenging fences faced by horses and jockeys alike as they make two circuits of the 2¼-mile-long course – although only thirty fences are ultimately jumped. Some of these are 'drop fences', where the landing side of the fence is lower than the take-off side. This means that the horses are unaware of the drop until they are in the air. However, the 'Chair Fence' has the opposite problem, because the approach side is lower than the landing side! Also, the horses have to negotiate some very tricky turns and then end the race with a 494yd run up to the winning post. This is why the famous Grand National is also notorious the world over as being one of the sport's most severe horse races.

A mystery surrounds the 1839 race: only three days before it was due to take place Lynn retired from organising the event and disappeared into relative obscurity. The reasons for this have never been satisfactorily explained, but control of the steeplechase immediately passed to a syndicate of wealthy aristocrats, brought together by Lord Sefton. This comprised Sefton himself; the Earl of Eglinton; the Earl of Wilton; Lord George Bentinck; Lord Grosvenor; the 13th Earl of Derby and his son, Lord Stanley.

The race meeting continued to grow in popularity and financial success, and in 1847 it was renamed once again, now as the Grand National Handicap Steeplechase. This is the name that it continues to hold officially today.

Up to 1949, the racecourse was owned by the Earls of Sefton, but in that year Lord Sefton sold it to the Topham family. Their matriarch, Mirabel Topham (born in 1891, and a former 'Gaiety Girl' dancer), became one of the most challenging, controversial and eccentric characters the racecourse had ever seen.

Running the Grand National and the Aintree racecourse from 1958 until 1973, Mrs Topham was passionate about racing, the 'National' and her racecourse. She built a second racetrack at Aintree within the established course and this opened in 1953.

This was at the same time as she opened a brand new motor-racing circuit around the perimeter of the course. This became renowned as one of the best racetracks in the world, being home to a European Grand Prix and five British Grand Prix, the first of which was won by Stirling Moss in 1955.

Mrs Topham was respected and loved by many race-goers and always provided good copy for journalists. Nevertheless, she was intensely disliked by many owners, some jockeys and by the BBC in particular. This was because Mirabel had her often forthright opinions and she stuck to them, right up to her death in 1980.

In 1973, Aintree Racecourse passed out of the hands of the Topham family and into those of the (some might say) notorious local property developer Bill Davies. He paid £3 million for the course, promising to continue to run the race even though he also had plans to build on some of the land. But Davis had actually borrowed some of the money to buy the course from the Tophams, so the financial arrangements were complicated. Also, he had no experience of running racecourses, so by 1976 the betting firm of Ladbrokes were in control of the race.

Over subsequent decades the racecourse passed through a variety of ownerships, with the Grand National itself being sponsored by an equally varied range of companies. Today, the Grand National is now run by Jockey Club Racecourses, and the racecourse is owned by a charitable trust, of which the current and 19th Earl of Derby is a trustee. The renowned racing novelist and jockey Dick Francis (1920–2010) was also a trustee until shortly before his own death.

Today, of course, the Grand National and Aintree continue to thrive, and the racecourse has five modern grandstands. Indeed, in 2007 the 19th Earl of Derby opened two of these, 'The Earl of Derby' and 'Lord Sefton' stands. (The last Earl of Sefton, the 7th, had died in 1972.) These are identical, spectacular, state-of-the-art, multi-purpose facilities, with outstanding views of the racecourse.

A number of exceptional horses have raced at Aintree but perhaps the Grand National's most famous was Red Rum. He came second in the National in 1975 and 1976, and won it in 1973, 1974 and 1977. His grave and a statue commemorating this extraordinary animal are both sited at the racecourse. Another record-breaker was Foinavon.

This horse, ridden by John Buckingham in 1967, avoided a massive pile-up at the course's smallest fence, cleared the obstacle and went on to win the race at odds of 100/1. The fence was later named Foinavon after the horse.

One of the most special races, however, was the 1981 event, when a previously un-fancied horse named Aldaniti was the winner. He was being ridden by Bob Champion (*b*.1948) who had recently recovered from cancer, and the cheers and tears of the crowds, and of the television viewers in their homes around Britain, as he entered the final run was a moving and uplifting experience for the entire country.

Aintree Racecourse has seen many victories and achievements, but it has also been the location for a number of less happy events. In 1993, and after two false starts, the race was abandoned and declared void, and for the only time in the history of the steeplechase. Some riders did not realise that the race had failed and completed the full two circuits of the course only to discover that they had all wasted their exertions!

However, it was the 1997 race that went down in history as the most difficult but also as a story of remarkable compassion and friendship. This was the year that an IRA bomb threat meant that the race had to be cancelled, and the 60,000 people at the course were evacuated. The National was postponed until the following Monday, but cars and coaches were impounded inside the course car parks overnight to allow them to be searched. This stranded over 20,000 race-goers in Liverpool, from all over Britain and the world. Many of these had little or no money or belongings as these were all in their vehicles, and they also had no place to stay overnight.

A local radio appeal went out to the public asking for volunteers to take in these temporarily homeless people. The immediate and positive response was overwhelming but unsurprising, as hundreds of Liverpudlians and Merseysiders threw open their homes. They provided free bed and board, laced with typical Scouse warmth and homely hospitality, for thousands of these people.

Despite these occasional difficulties, and though still a challenging race for horses and riders alike, the Grand National remains one of Britain's, and the world's, most thrilling and popular sporting events.

LOCKERBY ROAD AND THE FIJI ISLAND CASTAWAY

Just off Kensington, in the district of Fairfield in Liverpool, is an obscure street named 'Lockerby Road'. There seems to be nothing special about it, and it isn't even spelt like the name of the town in Scotland, which is ironic because it is named after a Scotsman. He was William Lockerby, who was born in 1782 in Ashbridge, Dumfrieshire.

William was a young sailor who had a very special dream. He wanted to sail to the South Seas because he had read so many books about this exotic part of the world, and these had awoken in him a passion to see so many wondrous things.

Natives of Fiji. (*LOC, LC-DIG-stereo-1s01762*)

He longed to see the vast expanses of the oceans that were sometimes brightest blue, as they reflected cloudless skies, but which could also become the deepest green, because of their immeasurable depths. He wanted to see for himself if porpoises and dolphins really did cut through the waves, and then weave in and out around the sides and prows of ships, guiding them towards new lands to explore.

William also wanted to find out for himself if it was true that fish could really fly. That they too would skim just below the surface and then suddenly leap out from the water, spreading out their fins like wings and gliding through the air and the tops of the waves. Did they then truly dive back below the surface again, all as the sun glinted and sparkled on their scales, turning them into a shimmering mass of rainbow colours?

He wanted to see the desert islands with their waving palm trees, which bore a mysterious fruit whose shell was as hard as iron but when broken open revealed a pure, white, sweet food and a delicious, nourishing milk. All of this, he had read, was bathed in the brightness of a tropical sky and caressed with warm breezes that bore the fragrance of strange new plants and flowers, yet blended with the clean salt tang of the South Seas.

Could it also be true that the people of those islands, and the maidens in particular, were of a stunning beauty? Did they really smile with such welcoming warmth, revealing the gleaming whiteness of their teeth? Were those smiles set in open and friendly faces, with dark eyes that seemed to draw you in, as if to bathe in a bottomless pool? Did the softness of their embrace and the texture of their flawless, sunbrowned skin make you feel as if you were being enveloped in the smoothest silk?

William needed to discover all this for himself and fulfill the dream he had held since childhood.

So, where would this young man – not yet 20 years of age – go to find a ship to take him to the other side of the world? To the greatest port in the growing British Empire, that's where: to Liverpool. Such was his determination that, sometime around 1806, he walked all the way, until he found himself in the crowded, bustling streets, docklands, and quaysides of the 'crossroads of the world'. He immediately paced the length and breadth of the quays, enquiring of each ship in turn:

'Master, where are you bound?'

'To the Americas, young Sir!'

'My friend, to where is your ship sailing?'

'To Spain and the Azores!'

'To where is your vessel bound, my friend?'

'To Botany Bay and Van Diemen's Land!'

None were sailing to William's destination, and day-after-day he returned to the wharves hoping all the time to hear the answer he desperately hoped for, but he sought in vain.

'Cannibal Tom', the last relic of Fiji cannibalism.
(LOC, LC-DIG-stereo-1s01755)

As he paced the seemingly endless waterfront of Liverpool, every morning he passed young Anne Curran as she sat on a capstan on the wharf. Only in her late teens, each day from this same place the softly spoken maiden, sold handmade love tokens and favours. Her fair fingers had made these for the loved ones of sailors to buy and then to give to their sons, husbands and lovers as keepsakes whilst at sea. What William noticed most about Anne was her face, which was as fair as her hands, as delicate as her demeanour and as comely as her slender figure. William and Anne were drawn to each other, and he told her about his dream.

As he waited, week after week after week it seemed, for a vessel to take him to the South Seas, the two young people got to know each other well, so well, in fact, that they fell deeply, and completely, in love. Even though they had known each other for such a short time, they married, in St Mary's Church, Walton-on-the-Hill. Even though too, Anne knew full well about William's vision of exploration and adventure, she supported him, encouraged him, and shared his disappointment that he could not find a ship to carry him to the South Seas.

Anne told him that when he did find a berth, as she believed he surely would, she would let him go. Although broken-hearted at his departure she would never stand in his way – her love for him would not allow her to. Anne assured him also that she would wait for him and would remain faithful and true no matter how long he was away, even if it took years for him to return.

'I will set sail my darling Anne,' he confirmed to her, 'but, when I do, I shall return a wealthy man, and we shall live together in comfort, security and love for the rest of our days.' His determination and conviction were certain, and Anne believed in him completely.

'Master, where are you bound?'

'To the Canary Isles, young man!'

'Sir, where are you sailing?'

'To the Carolinas!'

'To where is your vessel bound, my friend?'

'To the South Sea Islands, and we need hands – seek you a berth?'

Only a day later Anne stood on the Liverpool quayside and, after bidding her young husband a tearful farewell, and after he had released her from his devoted embrace, they waved goodbye to each other as

William's ship, *The Jenny*, drew out into the Mersey. From the great river, William sailed on to the Irish Sea, then to the Atlantic Ocean and onward into an exciting but uncertain adventure.

Anne waited for a year but there was no news of her husband or his ship. She waited for another two years but there was still no news. 'Come Anne,' her friends now began to say to her, 'you must recognise the truth of the situation: he must be lost, he is unlikely now to return to you.'

'My William is alive, I know it in my heart,' she retorted. 'He will return to me and will keep his promise.'

Anne waited for another five years, and her friends' insistence that she should marry again grew stronger. She was a woman on her own, still selling her love-tokens from her capstan on the quay. She had many suitors, but she turned them all down, trusting her heart, which still told her that William would return. In all, twelve years passed, never with any news of her husband, but Anne kept faith and remained true to William.

Then one day, as she sat on her capstan, a ship sailed in and tied up at the quayside. She paid it little attention, having been disappointed so many times before. But then she heard her name being called from the deck of the vessel, 'Anne! Anne, my love! It is me, your William. I have returned to you and my heart aches to be with you again.'

The lovers were reunited and their devotion for each other was undiminished, if anything it had been strengthened and deepened by their prolonged separation. Anne was as eager to hear about her husband's adventures as William was to tell her his tale. He explained that he had spent those long, lost years as a castaway, living amongst the cannibals of the Fiji Islands, who had adopted him into their culture instead of eating him!

He had turned his misfortune into an opportunity by establishing a trade with other islands and with passing ships in two commodities. These were the rare and exotically perfumed sandalwood bark and 'beche de mer', which is the boiled, dried and smoked flesh of sea cucumbers, a delicacy used to make soups. As a result William had made a vast fortune. The intrepid traveller also brought back and published his journal, recounting exciting tales of his time amongst the natives, telling of their habits and customs, and describing the thoughts of the very first white man ever to encounter these people and survive!

William was now able to fulfill all of his promises to Anne, and he became a successful shipowner and merchant. In 1847 he bought a large estate in Fairfield where he built Fairfield House between what are now Hollies Road and Lockerby Road. Here William and Anne had seven daughters and a son, and they lived happily and comfortably together until they both died, still devoted to each other and both in their seventies. All that now remains are William's story, the street and its name – Lockerby Road.

THE MASS GRAVES OF OLD SWAN

In the suburban district of Old Swan, to the east of Liverpool town centre, stands the beautiful Roman Catholic church of St Oswald. Designed by Augustus Welby Pugin (1812–52), it opened in 1842 and was the first Catholic church in the North of England since the Reformation to have been built with a tower and spire. It is also in St Oswald's that the first Roman Catholic Bishop of Liverpool, Bishop George Brown (1784–1856), is buried.

In the autumn of 1973, work began on excavating a plot of open land next to the church. This was to lay the foundations for new infant and junior schools to be attached to the church and to bear its name. However, just as digging was about to commence, the parish priest at that time, Father McCartney, warned the foreman that there might be some unmarked graves at one end of the site. So before any more work could take place, the Home Secretary had to sign an exhumation order. Then the mechanical diggers moved in.

With great care they began moving earth and, sure enough, an unmarked coffin was discovered at a depth of around 15ft (5m),

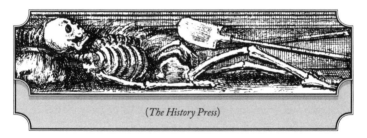

(*The History Press*)

soon followed by another one. With the greatest of respect, the workmen laid these side-by-side as digging continued. Then another coffin was dug up, and another, and another, as the digging process now speeded up. In fact, and to the amazement of everyone on site, and in an area of only around 40sq yds, a total of 3,561 coffins were eventually laid out in rows on the building site.

In fact, they were now being laid out above ground just as neatly and orderly as they had been buried beneath it, except that they had originally been interred up to sixteen coffins deep in places! This seemed to indicate that the burials had taken place as a single operation, but Father McCartney was as surprised as the workmen were. He had known anecdotally of one or two unmarked graves but knew nothing else about them at all. There were no written records of the burials in the church archives and certainly not of over 3,000 people!

I have heard one story, although how true it is I cannot say, that at one point during the hurried process of exhumation events took a particularly ghastly turn. It seems that as the coffins were being hauled up out of the ground, the perfectly preserved corpse of a young woman tumbled out of one of them. It was raining, and the ground was a muddy quagmire. The woman's body slid into the mud but, almost as soon as it did, her previously clear features began to disintegrate, as did the rest of her body. This horrified the men digging up the bodies, but it became worse as the rain got into more of the coffins. These now broke open too, emptying more decomposing and disintegrating cadavers in the mud, all around the horrified workmen. I have no information about how they dealt with this truly unpleasant turn of events.

Naturally, as soon as the first bodies had been discovered the Liverpool city coroner had been informed. But now came an urgent instruction, directly from the Home Office, to enclose the entire site with a 10ft-high secure fence with a locked gate. The site manager was also instructed that this was to be regarded as a restricted area and that no members of the public should be allowed on site. However, the exhumations were allowed to continue.

By this time, though, the press had got wind of the gruesome find, but they suddenly found themselves the subject of a D-Notice from the government preventing them from publishing any stories or pictures about the 'Old Swan Mass Grave'.

Soon after the instruction to erect the fence, another edict came from the Home Office, this time ordering the immediate cremation of the coffins and their contents, followed by the interment of the remains in an unmarked site in nearby Anfield cemetery. These instructions were carried out with great haste. Work on the new St Oswald's schools was halted for eighteen months whilst a complete pall of silence descended over the site and the story. Nevertheless, speculation was rife (although not in public) about the origins of the bodies, the circumstances of the peoples' deaths, and the reason for such a mass, unmarked burial pit.

As none of the coffins bore name-plates, one belief was that this indicated that the burial dated before 1840. This was because it was only after that date that registration of burials became compulsory and all coffins had to be identified. But this still left many questions unanswered.

Could these unfortunate people have been victims of the grisly Black Death, or Bubonic Plague, which had ravaged Britain, and especially Liverpool, throughout the Middle Ages and especially throughout the seventeenth century? This was unlikely, as plague victims' bodies were simply dumped, without coffins, in mass pits and covered with quicklime before being buried. Could they have been poor people from the Victorian slums of Liverpool, who had died in one of the many later plagues of the town, such as cholera, typhoid or dysentery?

The Old Swan burial pit. (*Discover Liverpool Library*)

If so, why are there no records of such an exceptional burial in the City Records Office?

Why were the Home Office so intent on hushing up the story and so determined to destroy the evidence quickly, especially before any post-mortems or samples could be taken for analysis and possible identification? The fact that all the coffins had been buried in such a methodical and orderly a manner showed that this had been a highly organised process. This implies the likely involvement of military personnel in the burials. Speculation continued, but soon life moved on. The schools were eventually built, and they are still open and happily serving the local community and parish to this day.

However, the story got a new lease of life in 1995 when some local historians contacted the Home Office for information about the burial pit. Even after over twenty years, a spokesperson for the government denied all knowledge of the case and said that as they had no records of the 'alleged mass grave' it was likely that this was all an invention of opportunist sensationalists or over-imaginative local people. But as there had been so many people present and involved at the time, this position taken by the Home Office had no validity.

To date the government still denies the existence of any records. Naturally, no detailed press reports exist, and I have only been able to trace one very poor photograph of the grave site.

Perhaps a more likely explanation is that these people had been Irish Famine migrants to Liverpool in the mid-1840s, who had been so weakened by starvation that they easily fell victim to Victorian epidemic diseases. Being only 'peasants', perhaps the Victorian authorities of the time simply buried them out of the way and saw no need to record either their identities or the fact of their interment.

Perhaps the reason for the subsequent official denials and obstruction is due to the politically sensitive nature of the times in which the bodies were discovered. During the 1970s tensions between Britain and Irish Nationalists were at such a bloody peak that bombs and other terrorist atrocities seemed to be happening virtually every week, both in Northern Ireland and on the British mainland. For the government of the day to admit that Irish people had been treated with such disrespect, even though a hundred years previously, would have provoked outrage amongst the Irish community with potentially violent consequences – if indeed this was the truth behind the mass grave of course. But this is simply my own speculation, for, as I have said, no official records exist.

Nevertheless, whatever the explanation may be for these anonymous burials, it is only right that we spare a kindly and respectful thought for those 3,561 unknown people in their unmarked graves and in their equally uncertain final resting place.

LIVERPOOL OBSERVATORY AND THE ONE O'CLOCK GUN

In 1834 the Royal Navy recommended that an astronomical observatory be established in the Port of Liverpool. This was because at that time the exact longitude of the town was unknown and there was little accuracy in the town's clocks. This meant that any of the thousands of vessels using the port every year who calibrated their ship's chronometer against any Liverpool clock would most likely have been incorrect.

As ships used their on-board chronometers to establish their precise latitude and longitude whilst at sea, they would often find themselves off course. There had been many instances of this in British naval history, when captains, thinking they were in open waters, sailed their ships into reefs or shoals, causing the ships to founder as a result.

The loss of life and property because of such errors was considerable, and this was not the sort of reputation that a great port like Liverpool wanted. So, taking the Admiralty's advice, the corporation of the town were happy to stump up the cost of a new observatory and of all the telescopes and scientific instruments that would have to go with it.

In 1845 the Liverpool Observatory was opened at Waterloo Dock, complete with a time-ball. This was a sphere which slid up and down a vertical pole mounted on the outside wall of the observatory. This was abruptly released to drop down the pole every day at precisely 1.00 p.m., Greenwich Mean Time. This was the same type of device as those that were already in use at Greenwich and Portsmouth. In fact, New York still drops a time-ball, in Times Square, to announce the New Year at midnight on each New Year's Eve.

The observatory after it was moved to Bidston Hill. (*The History Press*)

The accuracy of the time-ball was maintained using calculations made from tracking and timing the movement of the stars using a sophisticated 'tracking telescope' inside the observatory. Now ship's captains, or reliable members of their crew, would stand by the Liverpool time-ball ready to reset their chronometers as it fell, safe in the knowledge that these could now be trusted at sea.

The building of the observatory had fuelled an increased local interest in all things astronomical, and in the year of its opening a local brewer and amateur astronomer named William Lassell (1799–1880) designed and built his own 20ft-long telescope. He erected this at his home, and it was the most powerful telescope in Britain at that time. Lassell paid for its construction from the proceeds of beer that he sold to the labourers who were then digging what was to become the new Albert Dock!

Before long, his observations of the night sky resulted in him discovering Triton, a moon of Neptune, and Hyperion, the eighth moon of Saturn. He also discovered Ariel and Umbriel, two moons of Uranus, and because of his resulting national fame, in 1851 Queen Victoria (1819–1901) asked to meet with him during her visit to Liverpool. This growing fashion for astronomy led to the founding of the Liverpool Astronomical Society in 1881, and membership of this soon became worldwide, including, in due course, Dom Pedro II, the Emperor of Brazil.

In 1866 the present warehouse complex was to be built at Waterloo Dock, so the observatory and all its scientific equipment had to be moved. Its new home was in a purpose-built building on the summit of Bidston Hill, across the Mersey on the Wirral Peninsula. The staff there continued to observe the passage of the stars with the aid of the transit telescope, which was situated in the eastern dome of the observatory, thus still accurately calculating time. However, as Bidston Hill was now too far away for shipowners and captains to watch a visual time check, such apparatus as the time-ball became redundant. Instead, the One O'Clock Gun was established.

This came into operation on 21 September 1867, when a cannon that was relic of the Crimean War was fired from Morpeth Dock, Birkenhead, and again at precisely 1.00 p.m. every day. Now ships right across Merseyside as well as citizens of both Liverpool and The Wirral could hear the exceptionally loud 'bang' of the gun and set their watches to the exact time. The gun became quite a feature of Merseyside life for almost a hundred years.

The location of the cannon at Birkenhead was quite a distance away from Bidston, so it had to be fired remotely. Its ignition was triggered electronically by a specially adapted clock in the observatory. On the dockside, the cannon was loaded and tested at 12.30 p.m., and at one second to one o'clock, the switch would be thrown at the observatory and the signal would be sent down a wire to Morpeth Dock. On clear days the flash of the exploding cannon could be seen from across the Mersey.

Over the years a number of cannons served as the One O'Clock Gun, but the last one was a Second World War, 6-pounder, naval anti-aircraft Hotchkiss gun. Apart from a break during the war, the cannon continued firing until 18 July 1969. I remember it well, and it was so regular and so loud that, in fact, it became accepted as an everyday routine and yet was so normal that it was also easy to ignore. Even so, when the decision was taken to end the firings there was much disappointment on Merseyside, and it is still missed by those who remember it.

One of the earlier One O'Clock Guns is now on display at the Merseyside Maritime Museum, and William Lassell's own transit telescope is in the World Museum Liverpool.

WOOLIES

Frank Winfield Woolworth was born in New York in 1852. As a young man he trained as a clerk in a corner store in his home town, but in 1878 he set up his own 'Great Five Cent Store' in Utica, New York State, where he sold everything at that single price. However, his first business venture failed because of its poor location and so, in 1880, he set up a new store in Scranton, Pennsylvania. This was the first time that he put his name over the door of a store, in the distinctive gold letters of 'F W Woolworth & Co.' that were to become famous all over America and Britain.

Business boomed, and he soon added a ten-cent line of goods in the branches of his stores that were now springing up all over the USA, which soon became known as 'The Five and Ten Cent Store'. In the

Church Street, shown at around the time the first Woolworth's in Britain was built. (*The History Press*)

St Peter's before it was demolished to make way
for a larger Woolworth's. (*The History Press*)

early years of the twentieth century, Frank Woolworth had set his
sights on Britain, and he came here with his 'cheap and cheerful' concept of popular shopping.

He needed a very special location for his new store and, naturally,
he chose the retail centre of Liverpool for his pioneering premises.
Woolworth built his first British store in Church Street, in 1909,
on the site of what is now Goldsmiths Jewellers shop. At that time this
stood directly opposite the ancient church of St Peter's, which gave the
road its name. But, Frank Woolworth wanted a new and much bigger
store in Liverpool. Fortunately, this was at a time when Church Street
was being widened by the corporation, and St Peter's church was
demolished in 1922.

A brass Maltese cross, set in a granite slab in the pavement of
Church Street, still shows where the main door of this old building once stood. This now opened up opportunities for Frank, and he
commissioned a brand new building on the site of the church, which
still stands and which he named 'The Woolworth Building'. In the

pediment of this is another memorial to St Peter's: a carved relief of the crossed keys of St Peter.

Frank Woolworth died in 1918, four years before the completion of his new store, but this was destined to become the Woolworth Company's flagship shop in this country. Soon Woolworth's stores were opening up all around Britain, becoming known in Britain as 'Woolworth's 3d and 6d Stores'. Before long these popular shops were appearing in towns and cities all over the UK, to such an extent that, certainly by the 1960s and '70s, it was said that if a place did not have its own 'Woolies' then it was not a proper town!

In 2009, exactly 100 years after the founding of the first British 'Woolies', all the country's Woolworth stores closed down after the company failed and had to call in the receivers. A much-loved British institution had now come to a sad end.

MONKS ON THE MERSEY

In 1964 the Liverpool pop group Gerry and the Pacemakers recorded the song 'Ferry 'Cross the Mersey'. Reaching number eight in the British Top Twenty that year, and featuring in a successful film the following year, this was a sentimental tribute to Liverpool, the River Mersey and the Ferries. It is now the anthem of the modern Mersey Ferries, and it plays on board as passengers embark and disembark from the vessels. However, the origins of ferries across the turbulent river go right back to antiquity.

In fact, there have been boats on the Mersey for as long as people have lived here, probably since Neolithic Boat People settled here about 4,000 years ago. It is also likely that the Romans, who came to this part of Britain, may have been the first to use a ferry to cross the river, because remains of Roman roads have been found on the Wirral and also at Otterspool and Grassendale in Liverpool.

The word 'ferry' comes from an old Norse word *feryu*, meaning 'passage across the water'. This means that it is just as likely that the invading Vikings, who came here too, may also have needed a ferry. Indeed, considerable evidence of Norse settlements has also been found on both sides of the river.

Remains of the old Birkenhead Priory at the turn of the twentieth century. (*The History Press*)

However, in recorded history, the first known ferry service was provided by the monks of Birkenhead Priory, which had been founded in 1150 by Hamon de Massey (1129–1185), Baron of Dunham Massey. This religious order had established their priory on the shore of the Wirral Peninsula, on a promontory overlooking both the River Mersey to the east and a large, broad inlet to the south known as Tranmere Pool.

By 1160 the monks' ferry was operating across the Tranmere Pool, from the priory to a place called Rock House, from which comes the name of the local community of Rock Ferry. During the same period they also operated a ferry between Woodside, roughly where today's Birkenhead Ferry Terminal stands, across another wide inlet to the north called Bidston Pool. This landed at the tiny village of 'Seccum', thus giving modern Seacombe its name. So the first Mersey Ferries were actually along the Wirral sides of the river rather than across it to Liverpool.

Also around 1160, however, the Tranmere Pool began to silt up, and so the monks turned their attention to the tiny fishing village of 'Leverpul', across the often tempestuous waters of the River Mersey. They now established a ferry to this new destination. This was principally because they had built a mill and a corn warehouse on a cart track that would eventually become Water Street. This happened in 1207, when King John transformed the village by issuing a charter that created it as a new port, town and borough. He also ordered that seven streets be laid out, which still exist in exactly the same positions. As well as Water Street, these are Castle Street, High Street, Dale Street, Chapel Street, Old Hall Street and Tithebarn Street.

With the establishment of the new town the ferry began to get busier. However, although operated by the monks they had to lease the rights to do so from the reigning monarch, who actually held ownership. Indeed, King Edward I (1239–1307) visited Birkenhead Priory twice, in 1275 and 1277, and was impressed by its location.

As the monks were now crossing the river so frequently they realised that they could transport other people across too. They soon began to provide a ferry service to local travellers and for a fee were now rowing farmers, merchants and, perhaps, medieval tourists across the river. This ferry service became known as the 'Monks Ferry', a name that lasted for centuries even after the monks ceased operating it.

Because the small boats that made the crossings were mostly rowed across the river, sometimes using a small sail when conditions were suitable, the journey from Birkenhead to Liverpool could take up to one and a half hours on a good day and considerably longer if the river was rough. Indeed, the monks only attempted the crossing in fair weather, but they provided stranded voyagers with free food and lodgings at the priory until it was safe to cross. They also built and maintained free hostels on the Liverpool side of the river, adjacent to their mill.

As Liverpool began to grow, the monks found that, for the first time, they now had competitors for their ferry. Anyone could operate a cross-river service if they had a boat and were strong enough to row it. This was providing that they paid the fee for an operating license. Independent boatmen began to set themselves up along the riverbank, paying for their licences directly to the king rather than choosing to sublease them from the monks. This meant that these often unscrupulous operators could charge what tolls they liked and often swindled their passengers into the bargain.

In fact, there were so many complaints that there were frequent quarrels at the waterside. This led to a local official, the Boroughreeve of Birkenhead, issuing a warning to travellers not to pay a return fee in advance to boatmen, otherwise these tricksters might not wait for them to return, forcing these hapless people to pay another boatman to take them back across the river.

Because of this competition, by 1317 the priory at Birkenhead was in a very impoverished state, and so the monks petitioned King Edward II (1284–1327) for permission to build a large hostel in the priory grounds and also to begin charging travellers for their food and drink. Indeed, it is likely that in October 1323 this king visited the priory before taking the ferry to Liverpool. He stayed in the town for a week, residing at the formidable castle that once dominated the small but important port. But he was so disgusted at the poor state of Liverpool's seven streets that he instructed them all to be paved!

Fortunately, the monks received the king's permission for their new hostel, and because they provided a high quality, honest and reliable service, business soon began to grow again. So much so that in 1330 the monks then persuaded King Edward III (1312–77) to grant them a special royal charter to exclusively operate the ferry service. This king also gave the monks what they wanted, so they were once again the only legal providers of a ferry service across the river. Now they were very busy indeed and making money from the tolls they charged to transport passengers, their goods, chattels and, quite often, their horses and livestock too! Also, there were no more untrustworthy boatmen! In fact, no more competition at all!

This monopoly made the priory more solvent and generated sufficient income for the religious community to live quite comfortably for more than 200 years. Interestingly, this royal charter has never been revoked and, although the licence to operate ferries eventually passed out of the hands of the monks, most of the original terms and conditions still apply. This means that a special dispensation was granted through Parliament to allow modern ferry (and Mersey railway) tickets to be sold on either side of the river. This also applied to each of the Mersey Tunnels when they opened. However, today tunnel tolls are only charged on the Wirral sides of these great underwater thoroughfares.

In due course, however, along came the Reformation, during the reign of King Henry VIII (1491–1547), and so did the Dissolution of the Monasteries. In 1538, Birkenhead Priory was closed down by the king's troops, and the monks were forcibly evicted and dispersed. From that time the priory buildings, including the travellers' hostel, were allowed to fall into decay and ruin.

Whilst the ferry across the Mersey continued, the service was no longer operated by monks. In fact, the licensees of the ferries then passed through many different hands, including the Stanleys of Hooton, the Vyners of Bidston, the Molyneux family and also Ralph Worsley of Manchester.

A more modern pier was built at the monks' ferry site, and also many more river crossing points were established. This meant that, over succeeding centuries, ferries over the Mersey to Liverpool sailed from Ince, Runcorn, Ellesmere Port, Eastham, New Ferry, Rock Ferry, Tranmere, Woodside, Seacombe, Egremont and New Brighton.

The crypt of Birkenhead Priory in the seventeenth century.
(*Courtesy of Liverpool Athenaeum Library*)

The beach and piers at New Brighton on The
Wirral. The ferries can be seen at the end.
(*The History Press*)

Whilst the ferry services might have thrived, making the crossing
could still be a perilous undertaking. An early nineteenth-century
passenger on the old sailing ferry boats wrote of his experiences:

> The passage of the river, until steamboats were introduced, was a com-
> plete and serious voyage, which few undertook. The boatmen used to run
> their boats at one time on the beach opposite the end of Water Street
> and ply for hire. After the piers were ran out they hooked on at the steps
> calling aloud, 'Woodside, ahoy!' or 'Seacombe, ahoy!' And so on.
>
> It is a fact that thousands of Liverpool people at that time never were
> in Cheshire in their lives.
>
> We used to cross in open or half-decked boats, and sometimes we
> have been almost as many hours in crossing as we are now in minutes.
>
> I recollect once wanting to go to Woodside on a stormy day. The tide
> was running very strong and the wind blowing hard, and after nearly
> four hours hard work we managed to land near the Rock Perch, thankful
> for our lives being spared.

The ruins of Birkenhead Priory in the early nineteenth century. (*Courtesy of Liverpool Athenaeum Library*)

The old Birkenhead Ferry went out of use around 1872, and the 'Monks Ferry' pier was last used in 1878. However, the ruins of Birkenhead Priory survive, and they are maintained, preserved and open to the public, as is the location of the original monks' ferry. Many tales about this ancient religious community also survive, including one that tells of their lost gold.

The whole Wirral Peninsula is riddled with tunnels and caves, and a secret passageway is said to run under the priory ruins. As the monks were being violently evicted from their home during the Dissolution of the Monasteries, they tried to escape with large amounts of treasure down this underground passage. They were making their way along the passageway when a huge stone, which was balanced in the roof as a door, fell onto them. One monk was killed and the rest were forever entombed, with their gold.

The entrance was discovered in 1818, and the tunnel was explored for quite some way until it became quite blocked. Nevertheless, the passageway is believed to still run right under modern Birkenhead and to connect with the labyrinth of tunnels that are known to also exist under Wallasey and New Brighton. Many of these are natural, but parts of this subterranean network may also have been excavated by the monks and by later smugglers!

However, the monks' skeletons have never been found, and so their lost gold might still sit somewhere under Birkenhead, waiting to be discovered by some latter-day Indiana Jones!

THE OLD HUTTE

Despite the many wars that Liverpool and Merseyside have had to endure, and the frequent political and cultural upheavals that have afflicted local people over the centuries, we are fortunate that so many important historic buildings and houses have survived. Sadly, though, we have also lost many, and one of these was 'the Old Hutte', which was once the baronial house for the manor of 'Hale with Halewood'.

This local medieval community centred around nearby Hale, which still stands to the south-east of Liverpool, directly on the banks of the River Mersey. Hale had been awarded its royal charter as a township by King John in November 1203. This was four years before its neighbour, Liverpool, received its own charter from the same monarch,

The Olde Hutte Gatehouse pictured in 1810.
(*Courtesy of Liverpool Athenaeum Library*)

in August 1207. The township also, in the seventeenth century, had its own giant, who I tell of in 'The Childe of Hale – The Gentle Giant' on page 177.

Hale has always had its own lord of the manor, and it still does, although this role has much altered over the centuries. In 1285 Adam de Ireland (*b*?–1324), who held part of the Manor of Hale, married the daughter of Robert de Holand, Avina, who was the heiress to the adjoining Manor of Halewood. This then brought together the two sizeable estates and, in 1321, Adam bought the rights to the remainder of Hale Manor.

He was also the owner of the Hutte manor house, which appears to have been built sometime in the twelfth century. Records show that the Ireland family had established themselves there from around 1291, and this was their family home for over 300 years. To modern ears the name 'Hutte' might lead us to assume that there was something dishevelled, small and inconsequential about the house, but this was far from being the case. In fact, the word was originally Anglo-Saxon and meant 'home' or 'dwelling place', and the use of this name indicates that there was probably some sort of house on the site going back before the Norman Conquest of 1066.

This 'stately home' was a substantial mansion standing adjacent to three fishponds. It was set at the heart of woodlands at Halewood, just to the north of Hale, off a broad track that became known as Old Hutte Lane. Part of this survives as a short, narrow stretch of modern roadway.

Surrounded by a number of service buildings, the house comprised two wings running eastwards from either end of the main range. This contained the great hall, inside which was a spectacular fireplace, once said to have been the largest in Lancashire. As well as a yard, or possibly a garden, between the wings there was a main courtyard to the west of the main house.

Visitors to the Hutte and guests of the Ireland family made their way from Hale, and from the two tiny nearby coastal communities of Dungeon and Oglet, along Old Hutte Lane. From this track, and turning into the estate through a gate leading into the farmyard, a broad pathway then led to a stone bridge and causeway over a wide, water-filled moat. These are believed to have replaced an original drawbridge. Once across this obstacle, the entrance was through an impressive gatehouse that gave onto the manor courtyard.

The entire complex, which covered about an acre, was originally completely enclosed by the moat. This was fed by channels from the nearby Ram's Brook. Outside the moat, but still within the manor compound and to the west of the house, was the Hutte home farm with its own range of buildings. These enclosed a farmyard and comprised stables, barns, storage areas and lodges for carts and carriages.

Beyond all of the buildings was a long stretch of pasture that led to some woodland. Here there were pheasant runs, where the estate gamekeeper bred the birds for estate shooting parties. From the woods was a hidden pathway to nearby Hale Marsh, in the centre of which still stands the fascinating Hale Duck Decoy. The story of this remarkable pentagonal hunting lake is told in 'The Hale Duck Decoy' on page 95.

From the time they established themselves in the Hutte, the Ireland family became increasingly wealthy and politically powerful throughout Lancashire and further afield. Indeed, when Queen Elizabeth I (b.1533) died in 1603 leaving no children, the heir to the throne of England was King James VI of Scotland (1566–1625), who now also became King James I of England. In that year John Ireland (1558–1614) had become High Sheriff of Lancashire and, in that capacity, officially welcomed the monarch on his entrance into England. John then presented His Majesty with a loyal address, congratulating him on his accession to the English throne.

On John's death the manor and the Hutte passed to his brother, Sir Gilbert Ireland, who was MP for Liverpool. But, despite all the recent improvements, Gilbert did not like the ancient manor house at all. He did not find it grand enough for his family's rising status in the local community and in Britain. So in 1617 the foundations were laid for what was to become, in 1626, Hale Hall. This much larger and fully modern mansion house was constructed at the heart of Hale Township, in what is now Hale Park. Sadly, Hale Hall has also long since vanished.

Even though the Irelands no longer used the Hutte as a principal residence, the building seems to have undergone a second phase of improvements. This was because the Irelands and their descendants continued to find a use for the Hutte, as did the subsequent lords of the manor of Hale, the Blackburne family, perhaps as a guest or dower house. Indeed, the Hutte continued as an important focal point for the local community, from this time becoming known as 'the Old Hutte'.

Sadly, no paintings or images of the Old Hutte seem to exist, so we are dependent on written descriptions of the house to give us any idea of what it might have looked like. The building certainly survived beyond the seventeenth century, as did its gatehouse, farms, stables and a nearby group of estate workers' cottages. Nevertheless, with the Ireland family now living in their new home at Hale Hall, the Old Hutte became neglected and gradually fell into disrepair. Indeed, a fine east-facing bay window, thought to be part of a banqueting room constructed in the seventeenth century, fell into the moat in the early nineteenth century, so it seems to have become derelict by this time.

In the late nineteenth century an archaeological survey was carried out around the grounds and surviving buildings of the manor house. This described the Old Hutte in the past tense, which indicates that it had certainly been demolished by this time. The report described:

> ... a Great Hall, which would be a one storey building, and two wings, running out from the Great Hall in an easterly direction, each wing being two storeys high.
>
> The wing to the north would contain the solar, or withdrawing room, the knight's chamber, and the family apartments; and the southern wing the kitchens, offices, and servants' rooms.
>
> The Gothic archway formed the entrance to the Great Hall on its westerly side at the south end, next to the kitchen wing; and there would be a large wooden screen, partially shutting off the hall from the passage, which led through the south end of the Great Hall into the open space or court-yard at the easterly side, and also communicated with the kitchen.
>
> The Great Hall is traditionally said to have measured 100 feet long by 30 wide; the width is no doubt correct, but the length, there can be little doubt, included the solar and the middle chamber.

In fact, by 1960 all that remained of this once important baronial hall was the large Gothic archway entrance to the house plus the remains of the splendid fireplace from the great hall. However, there are no detailed records describing its final fate. Remarkably, though,

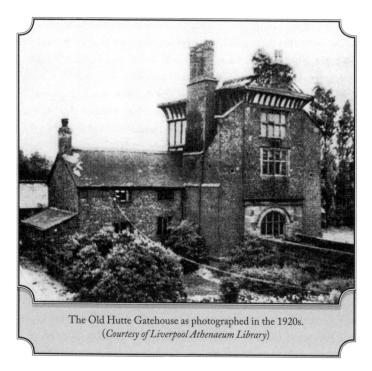

The Old Hutte Gatehouse as photographed in the 1920s.
(*Courtesy of Liverpool Athenaeum Library*)

the home farm, six small cottages and the substantial gatehouse to the manor compound had survived largely intact, if somewhat worn and torn by the passing centuries.

This building was narrow, stood three storeys tall and was built of a timber frame. This also underwent a series of alterations and modernisations over the centuries. Sometime in the late fourteenth century the eccentric structure had been converted into residential accommodation. Then, during the sixteenth century, mullioned windows and an imposing arched doorway had been added, giving it a distinctive Elizabethan character.

In the seventeenth century the original wattle and daub walls were all refaced in brick, and a tall, imposing chimney stack was also added. This served a new fireplace that had been built above the western half of the gate passage. 'John Irelande 1608' was carved upon its mantelpiece. In the eighteenth century a new brick farmhouse was added as an extension to the north side of the building.

Fortunately, a number of paintings and sketches survive of the gatehouse from this time, and these give it the appearance of something from the pages of a Grimm's fairy tale. Later photographs make it appear less fanciful but still charmingly unusual.

From 1935 the now quite sprawling gatehouse was occupied by a family named Burns, from Manchester. They worked the farm as tenants of Major Blackburne who was the last private owner of this Halewood estate.

By this time the gatehouse had become the estate farmhouse and had assumed the name of the original and long gone manor house. As a result, its tenants and the local community always referred to the gatehouse as 'the Old Hutte', often confusing some modern historians and archaeologists!

One of the last surviving residents of the Old Hutte estate is Elizabeth Dixon. She and her family lived in one of the old cottages, each of which, together with the gatehouse/farmhouse, remained occupied until the middle years of the twentieth century. I am indebted to Elizabeth for her recollections of life on the estate during the 1950s and 1960s and those of her family from earlier decades. She also generously provided family records, maps and photographs that have filled many gaps in my original research.

Elizabeth told me tales of visiting her neighbours on the nearby Whitfield Farm and the Lunt family farm where, as a child, she helped to churn butter by hand. Her vivid memories of weekly whist drives at the Lunt farm with family and neighbours, of wandering the surrounding fields and woodlands with her school friends, of collecting frogspawn from the moat, and of picking fruit from the farm's trees and watercress from the streams all conjure up a wonderful picture of mid-twentieth-century country life. So too do her recollections of riding on hay-laden carts during harvest-time, and of some local boys once stealing apples from the orchard and being caught in the act by her father. As a punishment the young scrumpers were made to eat them all, which was particularly harsh, as they had stolen cooking apples by mistake.

Elizabeth also tells of part of the gatehouse, and its tall chimney, being severely damaged by a direct hit from a Nazi incendiary bomb during the 1941 May Blitz. Whitfield Farm was also damaged in the attack, and 300 tons of hay were destroyed by the resulting blaze. All of this took place not more than a mile or two from the great conurbation of Liverpool and the industrial estates at Speke on the city's southern border.

However, in the 1950s a most important change befell the Old Hutte estate and its surrounding area when Major Blackburne sold the entire property to Liverpool Corporation. At first the authority considered completely restoring the gatehouse and the other surviving buildings and converting them into a folk museum. However, when inspectors were sent in to evaluate its potential for restoration they discovered that the old building was riddled with dry rot and would be far too costly to repair. It was then that the Ford Motor Company offered to buy the entire estate as part of the land that they needed for a new car factory.

And so in 1960 the Old Hutte gatehouse, the farm and its outbuildings, the cottages and the surviving estate were sold to the American car manufacturing giant. All the remaining tenants and farmers now had to move away.

In 1963 Ford (today Jaguar-Land Rover) opened their vast car assembly plant. They left nothing at all behind of the ancient estate. The moat and the fish ponds were filled in; the streams, fields, orchards and woodlands were ploughed up; and all the buildings, including the wonderful medieval gatehouse, fell prey to the bulldozers. Even a magnificent, gnarled giant oak tree, which for hundreds of years had stood immediately to the right of the causeway across the moat, was uprooted and destroyed.

Nothing at all now remains of the Old Hutte or its estate.

THE LEPERS' SQUINT

All Saints parish church in Childwall is the oldest surviving medieval church in Liverpool. Because of its listing in the Domesday Book, compiled for William the Conquerer (1028–1087) in 1086, it is clear that a chapel at least has stood on this site since the eleventh century. All Saints was always an important place of worship and it served ten local townships as part of its parish. These were Childwall, Hale, Halewood, Halebank,

Speke, Garston, Allerton, Much
Woolton (with Thingwall),
Little Woolton (now known as
Gateacre), and Wavertree.

Some archaeologists believe
that because of the layout
of the graveyard the church
could actually be Anglo-Saxon
in origin. This would certainly make it well over 1,000
years old. However, whilst
there are some pieces of Saxon
carved stone in the west wall,
and some Norman stonework
in the north chancel aisle,

Medieval leper.
(*Shutterstock, 98690135*)

the main structure of the present church building dates principally
from around the mid-1500s. The original church tower was replaced
in 1810, and the present roof dates from 1892. The parish records date
from 1557, which means that they are amongst the earliest surviving
local ecclesiastical documents in the country.

Entirely surrounding the church, and covering a large area, is its
graveyard. A wall that is itself quite old in sections, and in which
are set three lych gates, surrounds it. The oldest of these has the date
'1728' carved on its central column and it has been in continuous use
since that date. The word 'lych' derives from the old Anglo-Saxon
word *lic*, which means 'corpse'. It was under the lych gates that coffins
would temporarily rest on their way into the church and as the priest
performed the first part of the burial rites.

Until the establishment of private and municipal cemeteries in the
early nineteenth century, people could only be buried within the sanc-
tified grounds of a church. It was believed that the nearer your burial
place was to the altar then the better were your chances of getting into
Heaven. However, burials inside the building were reserved for senior
churchmen and aristocratic patrons, everyone else's grave had to be in
the churchyard.

Although the graveyard at All Saints is very much older, the first
written mention of it is in a document dating from 1386, and no

detailed records exist before 1557. The oldest tombstones at Childwall only date from 1620 and 1686, which is typical of such ancient churches. This is because inscribed stone grave-markers were very rare for ordinary people before the early seventeenth century. Any markers at all were usually only small, un-named wooden crosses. However, another reason why there are few earlier gravestones is that many churchyards hold more than one layer of bodies.

Even in small villages with an average population of only 250 inhabitants, at least several thousand people would have died and been buried each century. Graveyards could rarely spread outwards if they needed more space and this meant that they filled up quite quickly. However, even as recently as the early nineteenth century, graves were seldom dug deeper than 2 or 3ft. This meant that when a graveyard became full it was a simple matter to lay down a new layer of earth to the same depth. This then allowed new bodies to be buried above the earlier ones.

Over the centuries, however, this process might have been necessary more than once, which is likely to have been the case at Childwall. This is why people have to descend a set of steps to go inside All Saints church from its graveyard. Such multi-level burials also mean that there may be at least 20,000 bodies lying under the turf of even the most ordinary country churchyards.

There were, of course, certain members of the Christian community, especially before the Reformation in the sixteenth century, who were never allowed to be buried in churchyards: those people who were afflicted by leprosy.

Leprosy was common in England during the twelfth and thirteenth centuries in particular and especially in towns. The dreadful disfigurements associated with this highly contagious disease were seen by many as divine punishment for sin. Because of this people believed that there was the danger of moral as well as physical contamination, and so sufferers of leprosy were forcibly excluded from the community.

This meant that these unfortunate people had to establish their own settlements, or colonies. These often comprised men, women and children, because entire families would often develop the disease. Leper colonies were located well outside the villages and towns.

As a result, the infected community was almost totally dependent on the charity of others to survive. However, some more benevolent landlords would grant them land that they could farm or on which they could breed livestock. There was such a leper colony in Childwall Valley, adjacent to the Childwall brook and a large pond. This was a mile or so down the hill behind All Saints church and its graveyard.

If the lepers had to move around beyond their colony for any reason, they were required by law to do so in groups, and someone at the front would have to ring a bell and call out 'Unclean! Unclean!' This was to warn any people nearby to get as far away from the lepers as possible for fear of catching the disease and its 'moral corruption'.

However, lepers were still expected to attend church. In fact, most of them would certainly have wanted to, in the hope of salvation and freedom from this terrible sickness, if only in the afterlife. Of course, they were not allowed to sit even at the rear of a church whilst a service was in progress and were also denied access at other times.

All that can now be seen of the outside of the Lepers' Squint.
(*Discover Liverpool Library*)

Nevertheless, they still needed to make their confessions to the parish priest, hence the need for a 'Squint', or 'hagioscope' as it is known in architectural terms.

At Childwall the squint survives as what appears to be an arched window, recessed into the base of an outside wall of the church to a depth of about 18in. An open grill, about 12in sq, is set at the top of this recess, which looks directly into the rear of the church. Upon closer observation, though, this recess can be seen to reach down below the current level of the surrounding graveyard for a couple of feet. In fact, it is even deeper than this and was originally cut to accommodate an adult standing fully upright. The raised level of the graveyard now hides the rest of the recess, and it is only when one goes into the church that the original height of the squint can be seen.

On Sundays the congregation would make their way into the church, called by the sound of the ringing of the bells. At the same time the lepers would begin to make their way up the hill from Childwall Valley. Once the parishioners were inside the building the doors were closed, and only then would the lepers enter the church grounds.

They would then form an orderly queue outside the building and, one by one, would stand inside the recess and 'squint' through the grille. Standing inside the church was the priest, separated from the lepers by the wall, and he would hear each person's confession and offer absolution. Perhaps he might also have offered them some support and some hope. After the service the lepers would then make their way back down to their valley colony. Only once they had cleared the graveyard were the church doors opened, allowing the congregation to leave.

By the time of King Henry VIII's Reformation of the English Church, in the 1530s, leprosy had mostly died out in England. This was largely because of the forced quarantine of its sufferers. This also meant that the All Saints' squint was no longer needed, so it was eventually glazed over and left as a grilled window.

There are many reasons to visit the village of Childwall and especially its church and squint, both of which are certainly of considerable historical and social significance.

THE ENIGMATIC ELEANOR RIGBY

Who was Eleanor Rigby about whom John Lennon (1940–1980) and Paul McCartney (*b.*1942) wrote a hit song in 1966? Actually, she was no one special at all, at least not to history. However, she was a real person. Both John and Paul knew the village of Woolton well, which is a suburb of Liverpool and a place near which both boys had grown up. They had spent time playing here as children; later, as rebellious teenagers, they illicitly smoked cigarettes in the graveyard of St Peter's church, where Paul had been a chorister.

The name of Eleanor Rigby, wife of John Rigby, appears on a gravestone at St Peter's, and her name simply stuck in the boys' minds. They later recalled this when they were composing the song, but none of the incidents in their lyrics were taken from the life of the real Eleanor.

Eleanor Rigby's gravestone, in St Peter's churchyard, Woolton Village.
(*Discover Liverpool Library*)

On 3 December 1982 a sculpture was unveiled in the centre of Liverpool. Now standing in Stanley Street, this is a life-size representation, in bronze, of a park bench. At one end of this sits a thin and solitary woman, wearing a drab overcoat and a plain headscarf. This is the lonely 'Eleanor Rigby' from The Beatles' song, and she is feeding a couple of sparrows scattered on a crumpled sheet of newspaper. People can sit alongside the figure and, indeed, many visitors to the city do so to have their photograph taken alongside the famous character.

The sculpture was created by the 1950s rock and roll singer, and later actor, Tommy Steele (*b.*1946) and was unveiled by the sculptor himself. Sealed inside the bronze figure Tommy placed:

A four-leafed clover, representing luck;

A page of the Bible, representing spiritual help;

A football sock, representing action;

Copies of the *Dandy* and the *Beano* comics, representing entertainment;

And four sonnets for lovers.

Londoner Tommy said, 'I put them all inside the statue so she would be full of magical properties. I give Eleanor to Liverpool with an open heart and many thanks for my happy times in the city.'

The singer's sculpture of Eleanor Rigby is dedicated to 'all the lonely people ...'

BELLES, BEAUS AND CUPS OF TEA

Throughout the seventeenth century Liverpool, in common with most of Britain, had fallen prey to repeated outbreaks of a dreaded Black Death, or Bubonic Plague, which decimated the population of the country. By the opening decades of the 1700s people wanted to find places where nature was untouched by disease, preferably maintained

The famous Vauxhall Gardens, which inspired a
number of similar Liverpool attractions.
(*LOC, LC-DIG-pga-03193*)

in landscaped beauty and with walkways and watercourses through which they could freely wander in fresh and clean air.

In this way people began to feel reassured that mankind could, in fact, subdue and cultivate nature. This led to the creation of luxurious, private cultivated gardens and parklands, available to a paying public and with accompanying entertainment of only the highest standards and quality.

And so were born the 'Pleasure Gardens of Britain', which thrived throughout the eighteenth century and the early decades of the nineteenth century. The first of these, naturally, opened in London, but soon major towns and cities across the country had their own such gardens, not least of all Liverpool. We had the Spring Tea Gardens, close to where the Anglican Cathedral now stands; the Folly Gardens, on the site of the Wellington Column; and the most popular of all, the Ranelagh Tea Gardens.

Around 1759, a certain Mr Gibson opened and operated the Ranelagh Tea Gardens, which stood on the land between what are now Copperas Hill and Brownlow Hill. These were designed and planted behind what was known as the White House Tavern, also sometimes known as Ranelagh House. Inspired by Vauxhall Pleasure Gardens in London, Mr Gibson laid out, at considerable expense, landscaped gardens that were bounded by shrubberies and hedges. From the centre of his new gardens flowerbeds radiated out like spokes from a wheel and at its hub stood a tall, highly ornate Chinese temple. Inside this an orchestra played delightful music of the day, to entertain and divert the people who promenaded throughout the grounds.

Members of genteel society would meet at the Ranelagh Gardens. Beautiful and graceful ladies in their finest gowns, with hooped skirts, would seemingly glide along the pathways. Bonnets framed their pale faces and delicate lace shawls kept out the chill of the evening summer breezes. They would stroll along on the arms of their beaus, and these gentlemen were immaculately turned out in their neatly tailored suits with their double-breasted fronts, large buttons and flawless silk cravats.

Hundreds of flowers bloomed throughout the gardens, filling the air with heady and seductive perfumes. However, guests were discouraged from picking them by a sign that read:

You are welcome to walk here I say,
But if flower or fruit you pluck,
One shilling you must pay.

There were sculptured grottos set in wooded walks that ran alongside a lake and meandering watercourses. Surrounding the gardens were thickets of lilac and laburnum trees that sheltered hidden nooks and bowers. Here, lovers could 'plight their troth' (and other things) in seclusion and privacy, whilst the delicate tones and lyrical strains of the music wafted around the scene. The large pond had been stocked with a wide variety of fish that were so tame they came to the surface to be fed by the visitors. Indeed, some of the carp were so fat that they were too large to swim!

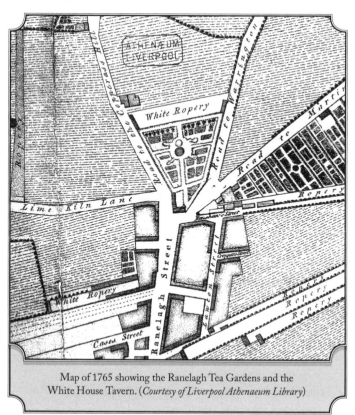

Map of 1765 showing the Ranelagh Tea Gardens and the White House Tavern. (*Courtesy of Liverpool Athenaeum Library*)

Liberally distributed handbills promoted all these features, as well as the firework displays, strawberry gardens and the rustic design of the buildings and ornamentation. Alcohol was not permitted as the gardens provided the glitterati of Liverpool 'with entertainment and diversions so admirably adapted for the consumption of tea'.

There was also a large concert room that could accommodate up to 1,000 people. Here, theatrical and dramatic productions were presented, musical extravaganzas performed, grand dinners held and exhibitions mounted. Elegant balls and concerts also provided the emerging middle classes of Liverpool with 'the most tasteful of cultural delights'. Special gala nights attracted hundreds of visitors, who would stroll, dance, picnic, imbibe copious amounts of tea, and canoodle in romantic and sensual privacy.

The Ranelagh Tea Gardens were still operating by the early years of the 1800s, but there seem to be no records of when or why they closed. What is known is that by 1826 they had disappeared and been replaced by houses. The White House Tavern had also been demolished and the very first Adelphi Hotel was built in its place. We shall hear more about Liverpool's own 'Grand Hotel' later.

Although they have now long gone, the name of the pleasure gardens lives on in Ranelagh Street, which runs down from Ranelagh Place, in front of the hotel. Even so, the pleasure gardens of Liverpool have not vanished forever, because they have been replaced by one of the finest collections of public parks, open spaces and recreation grounds in Britain. Liverpool is far from being the 'dark satanic mills' of common misconception, rather the city certainly is a 'green and pleasant land'.

THE MECCANO MAN AND DINKY DESIGNER

Three of the most popular toys of the twentieth century, in Britain particularly but then also around the world, were 'Meccano' construction sets, 'Hornby-Dublo' (Double 'O') model railways, and 'Dinky Toy' model cars and vehicles. These were all created by Liverpool-born Frank Hornby (1863–1936).

Frank Hornby's father was a wholesale grocery merchant in Liverpool, and the entire family were proud of their heritage; indeed,

Frank spoke with a strong Scouse accent all his life. However, Frank hated school, despite the determination of his parents to make sure he 'got a good education'. The boy played truant so much that by the time he left school at the age of 16, he found himself working in a series of poorly-paid clerking jobs.

Eventually he became a bookkeeper for a man named David Elliot, who owned a meat-importing company. Frank was happier here and got on well with his employer. However, he was unfulfilled and could not seem to settle. Nevertheless, the rest of his life was good, and by the late 1890s Frank married and went on to have two sons.

Frank Hornby.
(*Courtesy of Liverpool Athenaeum Library*)

He began to make toys for his young boys in 1898, in his garden shed, and built them metal models of lorries, bridges and cranes. He also created a working model of a submarine but whilst the craft dived perfectly, it failed to surface again. He was equally unsuccessful when he attempted to develop a perpetual motion machine!

However, never one to be daunted by such setbacks, and now discovering his real passion, Frank Hornby had a brainwave. This was to make his models out of miniature metal parts that could be fastened together with equally miniature screws and bolts. He also designed small spanners and screwdrivers to use on these components so that he could build whatever kind of model he wanted. His first design was a crane hoist, which originally used copper parts, but because this metal was too soft he later changed to using mild steel.

Early in 1901 Frank realised just how marketable this idea was, and his plan for 'Mechanics Made Easy' construction kits was born. For these he designed strips of metal, rounded at the ends for safety, half an inch wide and in three standard lengths. Each strip had holes drilled in it at regular distances so that they could be fastened together in a variety of ways, using his tools, nuts and bolts.

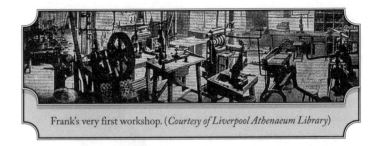

Frank's very first workshop. (*Courtesy of Liverpool Athenaeum Library*)

Borrowing £5 from his employer, David Elliot, Frank took out a patent, and in 1902 his first kits went on sale. These were produced in his Duke Street factory, which was actually only a small workshop above a shop. His manufacturing equipment consisted only of a single lathe, driven by a gas engine that sometimes worked and sometimes did not, and a couple of hand presses for stamping out the parts. Nevertheless, Frank manufactured a quality product, and each set came with enough parts to enable young people to create almost any toy they could imagine; however, to inspire and guide them, an instruction booklet was included with plans for twelve models.

A man of the times, Frank Hornby had never imagined for a moment that girls would be interested in his miniature engineering kits, so he aimed all of his products at boys. Sets first sold at 7*s* 6*d* (£30 at today's prices), so these were expensive toys only for serious young model-makers (with generous parents!). Even so, they proved very popular, and with the later addition of wheels, pulleys, axles, gears, bearings, brackets and face-plates, the range of creative possibilities proved almost endless.

By 1906, the new business was making a profit, and the 'Meccano' trademark was registered in 1907. The name is said to have been derived by Frank from the phrase 'make and know'. Then in 1908 the new Meccano Ltd company was also registered. It was at this point that Frank bought 5 acres of land at Old Swan and built his Binns Road factory.

Whilst Frank managed their company, David Elliot remained a silent business associate, and sales spread rapidly around the world. Soon they had branch offices and distribution centres in Barcelona, Berlin and Paris, as well as in America, and Meccano instruction booklets were being printed in fourteen languages!

After the end of the First World War the British Board of Trade suggested that Frank should consider making model trains and railways. He did so, and the first Hornby Clockwork Trains appeared in 1920, eventually, in 1925, developing into model locomotives driven by electricity. These were the first Hornby Dublo train sets, so called because they were '00' scale models, all beautifully designed and detailed, die-cast, and manufactured in high-quality tinplate. As with his Meccano sets, the train sets became popular around the world. In fact, by 1930 they were even outselling Meccano!

From 1916 the company had been publishing, also worldwide, the monthly *Meccano Magazine*. This continued until 1981, and copies of this are now collectors' items in their own right. By 1933 Frank Hornby was now selling his vast range of Dinky Toys. These detailed models, also die-cast but in zinc alloy, were not just of cars and road vehicles but also of farm vehicles, tanks and other military vehicles, boats and planes.

This new part of Frank's business became just as successful, because these models also became very popular collectors' items; they still command high prices today amongst expert collectors and enthusiasts alike.

The Meccano factory assembly line in the 1930s.
(*Discover Liverpool Library*)

Frank Hornby was a great believer in product diversity, so he went on to design and produce model village landscapes, buildings, tunnels and bridges for his train sets. He also created an extensive range of miniature furniture for dolls houses, so now he had something to offer to girls as well.

All of this international success made Frank Hornby an exceptionally wealthy man, but he wanted to make a wider contribution to society, so he served as MP for Everton from 1931–35. When he died, in 1936, at the age of 73, it was at the grand mansion that he had built for himself at Maghull, just north of Liverpool.

In 1979 the Binns Road factory closed and was soon demolished. A cinema and a sports and leisure centre now stand on the site. However, Meccano construction kits continue to be manufactured and sold around the world. After 1964 Hornby Trains passed through different owners but continues to survive as the separate Hornby company.

Long after the death of Frank Hornby, because both famous names are maintained, his legacy of imaginative and creative fun not only survives but is destined to continue for many generations to come.

Miniature Masterpieces

The very talented painter of miniature portraits, Sarah Biffin, was miniature herself, being only 37in tall. She had been born in Somerset on 25 October 1784 but without arms or hands. She also had only limited use of her legs and feet. Nevertheless, she painted exquisite, tiny portraits using only her mouth and shoulders, and she was also an expert needlewoman.

At the age of 12 her family apprenticed her to a travelling artist called Dukes. He agreed to develop her skills but, in return, she would have to travel with him on a sixteen-year

Sarah Biffin.
(*Discover Liverpool Library*)

contract, exhibiting her talents in a Freak Show. Sarah ended up in her own show booth, alongside the Fat Woman, the Human Skeleton and the Pig-Faced Lady, where she signed autographs and painted delicate miniature landscapes.

Dukes charged admission fees for people to watch her sew, paint and draw, but she also held her own exhibitions, at which she sold her paintings and signatures. Sarah also drew landscapes and painted miniature portraits on ivory, which were sold for three guineas each. But none of the money she earned was paid directly to her: it all went to Dukes who became very wealthy because of the tiny artist. Sarah was only paid £5 a year by him.

However, in 1812 her contract expired and so she was able to escape from Dukes' exploitative clutches. Sarah immediately made her way to London where she was determined to seek her fortune. Here she set up a studio in Bond Street where she quickly became a popular, fashionable and highly respected celebrity. At long last diminutive Sarah Biffin began to live a comfortable and secure life.

In 1821 Sarah's talent was officially recognised when she was presented with a medal by the Society of Arts. She was also patronised by King George III, George IV, William IV, Queen Victoria and many other titled and illustrious patrons, including the King of Holland. However, she wanted to improve her fortunes further. To do so she recognised that she really should travel to the place that was already being hailed as 'the most important town in the British Empire' outside London; so in 1842 Sarah Biffin came to Liverpool.

Now, and at the age of 63, Sarah held many exhibitions in the town, including one at the Collegiate School in Shaw Street, Everton. She continued to paint famous people, including the virtuoso violinist Paganini, on one of his many visits to Liverpool, and Charles Dickens (1812–1870) too, who refers to Sarah in his novels *Nicholas Nickleby* and *Martin Chuzzlewit*.

Sarah finally settled at No. 8 Duke Street in the town, and she continued to sell her paintings, but fashions changed and her fortunes waned. Money ran out, and she became dependent on a pension of £12 a year that had been granted to her by King William IV. The artist's eyesight began to fail and she became increasingly physically infirm. Fortunately, the wealthy Rathbone family, who were respected local philanthropists in Liverpool, arranged a public subscription that raised enough money to buy Sarah an annuity. Sadly, her illnesses overcame her and, only eight years later, on 2 October 1850, she died at the age of 66. Whilst most of her artwork was either lost or kept in unknown private hands, some of Sarah's miniatures survive to this day, and they really are quite beautiful.

Sarah Biffin lies buried in St James's burial ground, at the foot of Liverpool's Anglican Cathedral, but I cannot trace where exactly her grave is located – and I really have searched! However, inscribed on her tombstone are supposedly the following words:

> DESPOSITED BENEATH are the remains of SARAH BIFFIN who was born without hands or arms …
>
> Few have passed through the vale of life so much the child of hapless fortune as the deceased, and your possessor of mental endowments of no ordinary kind.
>
> Gifted with singular talents as an artist, thousands have been gratified with the able productions of her pencil, while her versatile conversation and agreeable manners elicited the admiration of all.

Indeed they did!

PLUMPTON'S HOLLOW AND THE LION IN THE WHEELBARROW

Between modern Boaler and Farnworth Streets, in the district of Liverpool now known as Sheil Park, was once an area of land called Plumpton's Hollow, and it was here that a temporary link was once made between Liverpool and Niagara Falls.

Set in a vale and bounded on all sides by high, sheltering embankments, Plumpton's Hollow was bought, in 1831, by Thomas Atkins. He owned what was then reputed to be the largest travelling animal show in the country. However, he had come to Liverpool to settle, with his animals, and so he had spent a fortune acquiring what was then a wasteland of gravel pits and dangerous ponds. He next set about transforming the Hollow into the Liverpool Zoological Gardens and opened it as a major public attraction in 1832.

Liverpool sea captains of his long acquaintance regularly supplied him with exotic creatures that they had brought back from the mysterious four corners of the world. This meant that Atkins' zoo was always well stocked with the most curious animals, all of which were new to his delighted customers.

Inside the very large central menagerie building were various mammals, birds and reptiles. These included large carnivores, such as wolves and leopards, and visitors could also see specimens of the now extinct quagga, which was a partially striped subspecies of zebra. There were also huge lion and tiger crossbreeds, now known as ligers, which average 10ft (3½m) in length and can weigh up to 50st (318kgs).

Rajah the elephant was a very popular creature at the zoo as he gave rides to the children on his back. However, he killed his keeper and was shot. His body was then boiled to remove his flesh. All of his bones, including his great tusks, were then piled up and put on display. Atkins was never a man to pass up a money-making opportunity.

The grounds had been very attractively landscaped as beautiful pleasure gardens. With winding pathways across well-kept lawns, passing ranges of colourful flowerbeds, patrons could explore mazes, test their skills on an archery ground, visit the 'hydro-incubator', in which chickens were being 'continually hatched by steam', and see a full-scale replica of Shakespeare's house in Stratford-upon-Avon. To further entertain his paying public, Atkins provided musical concerts in what he had named his 'Musical Temple', as well as balloon ascents and fireworks displays.

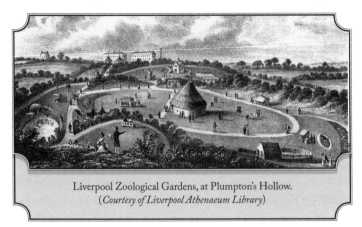

Liverpool Zoological Gardens, at Plumpton's Hollow.
(*Courtesy of Liverpool Athenaeum Library*)

It cost 1*s* to visit the gardens, which was quite expensive for the time, but people could also buy season tickets for a guinea, which gained them admission for a year. The zoo became so popular that visitors came in their thousands, not just from Liverpool but from all over the region.

To keep paying customers returning for more, Atkins also booked the best performers and novelty acts of the day, which is where the Niagara Falls connection was made, in the person of Charles Blondin (1824–1897).

Born in France in 1824, this exceptionally skilled tightrope walker had become one of the best known aerial acrobats of all time because of his always spectacular and dangerous feats. Blondin's greatest stunt to date had been in 1859 when he crossed Niagara Falls

Blondin.
(*Discover Liverpool Library*)

on a tightrope. He then did it again, only this time blindfolded, wheeling a barrow, twirling an umbrella and carrying his manager on his back! This feat guaranteed him world fame, and he made a fortune by repeating it on highwires all over the globe, especially in England.

Now he was one of Atkins' top-line celebrities at Plumpton's Hollow, where he made his first appearance, in 1860, to great local acclaim. When he returned to Liverpool and the Zoological Gardens in 1863, however, he knew he would have to do something especially astounding to again win the approval of what was always a very tough audience: Liverpudlians had seen just about everything by this time!

So now Blondin crossed a highwire that had been stretched directly above the upturned heads and open mouths of hundreds of astounded Scousers. As they looked up aghast, along the tightrope the acrobat pushed a live male lion, strapped into a wheelbarrow. However, this incredible exhibition almost ended in disaster because a guy-rope became entangled around the barrow wheel. The tightrope walker, and his potentially ferocious companion, almost slipped and fell into the enormous crowd below.

However, Blondin recovered his balance and continued his performance safely, to the roared approval of the spectators – if not the lion.

A particularly spectacular attraction at Plumpton's Hollow was the Centrifugal Railway, which ran from the top of a tower standing about 20ft high. As a contemporary writer described:

> … from this a substantial car, to hold one person, was dispatched down a steep decline, whence the vehicle was hurried round a ring, from which it was projected up an incline, from the crest of which the car speedily ran round the gardens on a rail back to the tower base. This apparently dangerous journey was in fact a safe one with common care. The railway was made of the best material, and accidents rarely if ever took place. Behind the railway tower was the monkey cage.

In this primate enclosure were a series of separate cages for smaller animals, plus a larger one for the chimps and orang-utans. Nearby, a large lake had been constructed for all kinds of waterfowl, the most popular of which were a pair of pelicans, which were described as 'always looking particularly dejected'.

There was also a large bear pit, with a tall central pole. Visitors were actively encouraged to 'feed the animals', and they held out cakes to the bears. The large animals would then climb the pole to try to get the cakes as a reward for their entertaining efforts. However, if the animal fell from the pole, which happened frequently, this provided the spectators with even greater amusement – values were very different then.

One particularly large bear, no doubt after severe provocation, actually managed to escape from the pit and the zoo grounds, making his way onto nearby West Derby Road. The confused and terrified creature was pursued by crowds of people, so he occasionally stopped his desperate dash to turn and confront them. Naturally, following the accepted behaviour of the time, this provided the people with an opportunity to pelt him with whatever came to hand, so off he would charge again.

No one dared approach the animal except for William Mayman. He was the landlord of a nearby pub known as The Parrot. Mayman already had a connection with Atkins' zoo, because he had once been a keeper there. He had become a local hero when he rescued a young boy who was being mauled by, ironically, an escaped bear. The large financial reward he received for this act of courage had enabled him to buy the pub.

Now the courageous publican approached the bear and tried to subdue him simply by strength: Mayman was a large and powerful individual. However, the bear did not want to come quietly and, in the process of eventually being subdued and captured, tore a great gash in the landlord's arm. This was so bad that Mayman had to have his arm amputated.

Nevertheless, upon his recovery, Mayman saw a commercial opportunity. He re-licenced his pub as The Man and Bear and commissioned a new pub-sign showing him and the animal. This bore the text 'Mayman in the jaws of the bear'. For quite some time this increased the number of drinkers in the pub and Mayman became a celebrity. The pub stood on the corner of Hygeia Street and West Derby Road, but has long since been demolished.

Records show that Thomas Atkins left Liverpool sometime in the 1850s but they don't specify why or when. However, in 1859 the zoo was sold to a group of private investors, and it became a shareholding company under the name of The Liverpool Zoological Gardens Co. Ltd. By this time, and to boost public interest in what was now becoming a fading novelty, a spirit licence for the zoo had been acquired and two drinking saloons had been built.

However, these now began to attract an entirely different type of visitor to the zoo and gardens. Soon the pleasure grounds were being described as the regular haunt of drunkards, ne'er-do-wells, and youths of wantonness and questionable morals! The more discerning paying public stayed away, and in 1863 the company went bankrupt. The land was bought by Liverpool Corporation, who cleared away the old zoo and pleasure ground buildings soon after. They built Boaler, Goldsmith, Bourne and Empire Streets on the site.

Nothing now remains of Plumpton's Hollow or of Thomas Atkins' renowned zoo and gardens. The area is still a large housing estate, and the only claim to fame it now has is that here can be found George Harrison Close, Paul McCartney Way, Ringo Starr Drive and John Lennon Drive.

WHO REALLY CONQUERED MOUNT EVEREST FIRST?

Everyone knows that Sir Edmund Hillary (1919–2008), accompanied and guided by the remarkable Tenzing Norgay (1914–1986), a Nepalese Indian Sherpa mountaineer, were the first people to climb to the summit of the world's highest mountain, Mount Everest in Nepal. They reached the 29,029ft (8,848m) summit on 29 May 1953 – or did they?

In June 1924 a British expedition set off to climb Everest, led by Andrew Comyn Irvine and George Leigh-Mallory. However, and in mysterious circumstances, both men died on the summit of the great peak. Nevertheless, many people now speculate that perhaps Irvine and Leigh-Mallory actually made it to the summit, almost thirty years before Hillary and Tenzing.

Andrew 'Sandy' Irvine was born in Birkenhead in 1902 and had been educated at Birkenhead Preparatory School and Birkenhead Junior School from 1910–16. He then completed his education at Shrewsbury School. George Leigh-Mallory was born in 1886 in Mobberley, Cheshire, and his father was the vicar of St John's church in Huskinson Street, off Grange Road, also in Birkenhead.

It was at 12.50 p.m. on Sunday, 8 June 1924 that Noel Odell (1890–1987), a member of the Everest team, saw the distant figures

of his companions, Irvine and Mallory, on the North East Ridge of the mountain and within striking distance of the summit. Odell was following his teammates up the peak and was several thousand feet below them. His task was to prepare the camp for the two climbers for their return journey, following what was confidently expected to be their successful conquering of the great mountain.

Mount Everest.
(*Shutterstock, 175336589*)

Odell had a clear view of his fellow climbers but only as tiny specks high above him on the mountainside. Then a great bank of cloud flowed in, completely enshrouding Irvine and Leigh-Mallory and obscuring them from Odell's view. After the expedition, Odell wrote:

> There was a sudden clearing above me and I saw the whole summit ridge and final peak of Everest unveiled.
>
> I noticed far away on a snow-slope ... a tiny object moving and approaching the rock step. A second object followed, and then the first climbed to the top of the step. As I stood intently watching this dramatic appearance, the scene became enveloped in cloud.

This was the last time that Irvine and Leigh-Mallory were ever seen alive. However, and inevitably, the question has remained ever since: did either or both of them make the summit twenty-nine years before Hillary and Tenzing Norgay? This was never satisfactorily answered and the mystery remains.

Over the years, a number of expeditions have been mounted to try to discover what happened to the ill-fated climbers, and in 1999, on what was the seventy-fifth anniversary of this disastrous mountaineering attempt, an Anglo-American team retraced the route of the 1924 British Everest expedition. They found George Leigh-Mallory's preserved remains, 2,000ft from the summit.

The body of the unfortunate mountaineer was described as being in a remarkable state of preservation and was simply lying partially buried in the snow. They described the exposed flesh of the climber as being 'ivory white, smooth, and hard' and suggested, from the position of the corpse, that he may have fallen. One leg was certainly broken and the shoulder was injured. The implication of this was that Leigh-Mallory may well have lain on the snow following his fall, unable to move and simply waiting for his inevitable death. However, did the climber die on the ascent or on the descent? Tantalizingly, there was no evidence to confirm whether or not either of the climbers had actually reached the summit of Everest.

But what of his companion? The body of Irvine has not, as yet, been discovered, and there were no signs of him anywhere near Leigh-Mallory's body. It was known that Sandy Irvine had taken a camera with him on the climb, but neither this nor his body have ever been found. The Birkenhead climber lies there still, somewhere high on the roof of the world amidst the ice, snow and cloud, perhaps with the photographic evidence that would settle the question once and for all.

George Leigh-Mallory's remains were left exactly where they were found on the mountain. This was partially out of respect but also because it would have been far too difficult and dangerous to attempt to bring it down. In fact, the bodies of well over 200 climbers lie near the summit of Everest; each of these was killed in attempts to reach the top of this formidable and perilous mountain.

So the question still remains, at least for the time being: were Hillary and Tenzing or the two mountaineers from Birkenhead the first to climb Mount Everest successfully? Perhaps we shall never discover the truth. However, three roads off Borough Road in Prenton were named to commemorate the intrepid though tragic Wirral climbers: Mallory Road, Irvine Road and Everest Road.

THE GUINEA GAP TREASURE TROVE

Most people know of the public swimming baths on the Seacombe waterfront, named Guinea Gap Baths, but they might not know that this is the oldest public swimming pool on the Wirral. Costing £15,000 to build, it was opened on 7 April 1908, and from 1908–57 205 national and world swimming records were set at the baths.

Although it later had a very sophisticated filtration and heating system installed, originally the water was pumped into the pool directly from the Mersey. This meant that it was not only very cold but was permanently a murky-brown colour!

But why was it called the Guinea Gap? The name comes from a natural cleft, or gap, that had formed in the high embankment above the river, sometime in the early eighteenth century following a storm. The gap is still there but is now a paved pathway from the road down to the modern esplanade that runs along the Wallasey waterfront. However, when the gap first opened up it also created a large natural basin against the shore. This was big enough for a number of people

Seacombe Promenade, built over Guinea Gap – where a
treasure hoard was found in 1850. (*The History Press*)

to swim safely in at low tide. This proved to be very popular indeed,
and local boys came here regularly to strip off and frolic about in the
river waters.

But in around 1850 one of these youngsters felt something round and
hard beneath his foot in the sand under the water. When he lifted up
his leg to see what was caught between his toes, he, and his very excited
friends, saw a golden guinea. This bore the head of King William III
(1650–1702), so dated from the end of the seventeenth century.

The boys now scrabbled around in the sand, where they discovered
around fifty of these valuable gold coins. As a result, the gap soon
became known as the 'Guinea Gap', and the coins were believed to be
some of the hoard of the local smuggler chieftainess, Mother Redcap.
Her isolated tavern had stood for very many years further along the
coast at Egremont, where a large treasure had always been believed to
have lain undiscovered.

What happened to the gold coins is not known; there are no records
stating into whose pocket or bank account they eventually found their
way. It is almost certain that the boys who found them didn't get to
keep them, so all that remains of this curious incident today is the
Guinea Gap itself.

HUYTON INTERNMENT CAMP

During the Second World War, in May 1940, the British Home Secretary ordered that all Germans and Austrians between the ages of 16 and 60 then resident in Britain should be interned in special camps as 'enemy aliens'. This was because of the fear of spying or sabotage being carried out in Britain by foreign enemy nationals and Nazi sympathisers. This policy involved the immediate imprisonment of around 27,000 people, mainly men and boys but also a significant number of women and girls. Males and females were housed in separate camps, often in different parts of the country, so many families were split apart by this system.

Just to the east of Liverpool is the small town of Huyton, then part of the Borough of Liverpool, and this district was selected as the location for one of these internment camps. The Huyton Camp did not involve the building of any special structures but simply consisted of a number of streets of newly built but otherwise empty council houses, commandeered by the War Office. These streets were then enclosed by an 8ft-high barbed-wire fence.

The new houses had been built by Liverpool Corporation as an overspill housing estate, but now sentries with guard dogs patrolled its perimeter, which was punctuated by high watch towers placed at strategic points. These were manned by guards armed with machine guns who, at night, swept the camp with searchlights mounted on platforms. This large compound was, in fact, a fortified prisoner-of-war camp in all but name.

Originally intended to simply be a transit camp, it actually remained in place from May 1940 to October 1941. Up to 5,000 enemy alien detainees were held here whilst awaiting transfer to Australia, New Zealand or Canada, or to the more permanent internment camps that had been set up on the Isle of Man. However, on 2 July 1940 the Cammell Laird-built Blue Star liner *Arandora Star*, carrying mostly German and Italian detainees from Liverpool to Canada, was torpedoed and sunk off the coast of Ireland with the loss of over 800 lives. As a result of this tragedy overseas deportations were brought to an end.

There were two camps at Huyton: Camp One, comprising the initial housing estate, with at least twelve people billeted to each house, and Camp Two, which consisted of tents pitched on adjacent waste-land. There were four people to each tent, and when it rained the ground became flooded and mud-washed. Conditions quickly became extremely uncomfortable and unhygienic.

In fact, from the time that it opened conditions at the Huyton Camp had been extremely poor.

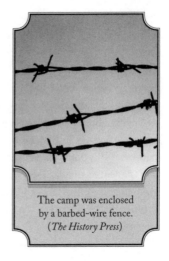

The camp was enclosed by a barbed-wire fence. (*The History Press*)

One of its biggest problems was that it was seriously overcrowded. This was because so many people were being confined in the houses but only 140 beds were available to them. In fact, many of the houses had only been partly built and were without windows or completed roofs or walls. Most people had to sleep on the floors and tables or on whatever other suitable furniture there was. Many were sick and incapacitated and had to be left on bedding or spare mattresses in overfull rooms.

Many internees were mentally ill or physically handicapped and needed constant care and support. This they only received from their fellow inmates because, at first, there was only one medical officer for the entire camp. Later, a number of internees with medical degrees worked with this dedicated and tireless British soldier to allevi-ate the suffering of their fellow prisoners. Diaries, secretly kept by some of the inmates, showed that some, but not all, of the conditions gradually improved.

Undoubtedly, some internees were indeed Nazi supporters but, sadly, most were actually refugees from Hitler. Many had already been subjected to brutal persecution on racial or political grounds, and a sig-nificant number were Jews who had come to Britain to seek safety and asylum in a free country. The irony and anguish, therefore, of finding themselves in what amounted to a concentration camp must have been appalling. Now they found themselves in humiliating and unpleasant circumstances and separated from their loved ones. This made their incarceration much more stressful and hard to bear, but at least they had escaped the brutality, the torture and the gas chambers of the Nazi regime.

Amongst a number of prominent internees was the Austrian composer Hans Gal (1890–1987), who wrote his 'Huyton Suite' whilst a prisoner in the camp. He composed this for a flute and two violins, which were the only instruments then available to him. There were also

Winston Churchill, whose investigation of the camp brought about real improvements to the internees' situation.
(*LOC, LC-USZ62-64419*)

two young artists, Walter Nessler (1912–2001) and Hugo Dachinger (1908–1995), who painted scenes of camp life on old newspapers and wallpaper. Examples of the work of both artists are in the collection of the Walker Art Gallery in Liverpool city centre.

People from all over Britain were shipped to Huyton to be imprisoned in what was one of the largest such camps in the country, and they were kept there until they could be proved to be no threat to the war effort. However, it could take months or, in some cases, even years to confirm the innocence of many of these internees so that they could be released. Most people in Britain's internment camps had been released by the end of 1942, but the last were not freed until the end of 1945, well after the war had ended.

The people of Huyton were angered and ashamed by what was taking place in their community, and they smuggled food, clothes, shoes and blankets in to the prisoners who were, in effect, their neighbours. They also complained bitterly to the government about the way these people were being treated, and in August 1940 Prime Minister Winston Churchill (1874–1965) ordered a thorough investigation of the camp and its management. He was appalled when he was presented with the report and ordered a wholesale improvement of the internees' conditions. His instructions were immediately carried out.

In fact, by early 1941 most internees at Huyton had been freed and by October of that year the camp had released all of its inmates. The site was then used as a military facility until the end of the war, when building work on the houses was finally completed and it became the housing estate that is now known as Woolfall Heath.

The story of the Second World War internment camp at Huyton is one that shows the wartime government of Britain in a very bad light but reflects very well on the people of Huyton – true Scousers who understand and object to injustice and will always fight it.

THE STORETON DINOSAURS

The ancient quarries at Storeton on the Wirral are an important historical site and provided stone for around 2,000 years. They were originally up to 200ft deep in places but are now disused and overgrown with woodlands. However, it was the Roman invaders who first excavated here, in the first century AD, to find stone for their local buildings. The quarries remained in use well into the twentieth century, when a Victorian tramway was still being used to transport stone throughout the area and to the docks at Bromborough Pool.

The quarry itself was largely filled in though in the 1920s, with the excavations from the Queensway Mersey Tunnel, and the whole area is now a very popular nature reserve. The old tramway has virtually disappeared too, buried under the playing fields of Wirral Grammar School and various housing developments. In fact, Quarry Road and Quarry Road East in Bebington still follow the route of this old transport system, although part of it has been reconstructed as a historic feature.

The former quarries were also important archaeologically. This was because it was here that some of the very few traces of Merseyside before the Ice Age were found. In the nineteenth century quarry-men began to discover sets of fossilised animal tracks in the slabs of stone they were cutting, and palaeontologists later identified these as belonging to a prehistoric creature called a Chirotherium.

In the Triassic period, around 250 million years ago, which was the beginning of the 'Age of the Great Reptiles', what is now Merseyside was prowled by this dinosaur. Its name means 'Hand Beast' because of the five-fingered shape of its fossilised footprints. This great lizard measured about 2.5m long, stood around 1.5m tall and had a slim but muscular body with a long, powerful tail. It may have been amphibious and perhaps a relative of the crocodile, because it had long rows of strong, sharp teeth and was undoubtedly carnivorous. A life-size model of this creature is on display in the World Museum Liverpool.

Slabs with the preserved footprints are also on display in the museum as well as in the Williamson Art Gallery in Birkenhead. Other footprints of the Chirotherium can still also be seen, at certain times, on the shore at Crosby, just to the north of Liverpool, but the best local examples came from Storeton. Indeed, throughout the nineteenth century finds continued to be made here and, as a local curiosity, some of these were built into the porch of Bebington church. Sadly, though, many of the best finds were destroyed during the May Blitz in 1941. This was when Liverpool Museum was almost completely destroyed by German bombing. Fortunately, enough samples survived to tell us something of our very ancient past.

What has also been learned is that the 'Hand Beast' was not the only local dinosaur, because we also had Rhynchosaurs, which means 'Snouted Lizard'. This creature was a herbivore with a long, hooked beak for grubbing up roots. It also had powerful jaws and strong teeth for tearing down and chewing tough plants. Rhynchosaurs were also large, about 1m high and 2m long, and they must have been very heavy to have left such deep and lasting footprints in the mud of prehistoric Merseyside. This animal may have been powerfully built but, unfortunately for the Snouted Lizard, it was the main food supply of Chirotherium!

Whilst our local dinosaurs may not have been truly spectacular monsters, like T-Rex or Brachiosaurus, they were certainly formidable enough and show that life of one form or another has been around on Merseyside for a very long time indeed!

Storeton Quarry as it appeared in 1933. (*Discover Liverpool Library*)

REYNOLDS' WAXWORKS – FREAKS, FRIGHTS AND FANTASIES

One of the longest-standing and most popular attractions in the North of England was Reynolds' Waxworks and Exhibition. This opened in 1858 at No. 12 Lime Street in Liverpool, directly facing the entrance to the station. Owned and operated by Alfred Reynolds, and later by his son Charles, this was based on Madame Tussaud's Waxworks in London. However, Alfred was determined to offer much more sensational subject matter, which would appeal to the thrill-seeking and perhaps jaded tastes of nineteenth-century Liverpudlians. In fact, Reynolds ensured that his exhibitions became increasingly bizarre.

This guaranteed the continuing popularity of his waxworks and prompted a sudden increase in other such attractions on the street, each trying to cash in on the craze for the weird and the horrifying. This included the Tivoli Palace of Varieties, which once stood on the opposite corner of Lime Street to the Vines pub. According to a photograph I have, this advertised an appearance by John (Joseph) Merrick (1862–1890), the 'Elephant Man'. However, Reynolds' Waxworks and Exhibition always had the edge!

This was because one of his most lurid attractions was an extensive exhibition of actual-size, wax anatomical models. These illustrated, in full colour, what advertising described as 'the fruits of sin and the consequences of uncleanliness'. There were highly detailed models of particularly intimate body parts showing the symptoms of syphilis and gonorrhea. As a result, queues to see this collection would regularly stretch out into the street.

To add to his portfolio of macabre exhibitions, Reynolds also opened a Chamber of Horrors. His promotional handbills and posters were seen all over Liverpool and beyond, announcing chilling wax models and tableaux of 'murder most foul' and 'representations of torment and terror'!

The opening hours were 10 a.m. until 10 p.m., and admission cost 3*d* to view the displays but 6*d* if you wished to see the live exhibitions and entertainments as well, which were performed twice a day at 3 p.m. and 8 p.m. These shows were billed as being 'of a sensational and horrifying character' and included a 'Flea Circus' and 'Freaks of Nature', such as 'The Norwegian Giant' and 'Tiny Tim', who competed with General Tom Thumb from Barnum's Freak Show, which was then touring the world and had visited Liverpool. There was also 'The Infant Jumbo', who was billed as 'the most wonderful child ever exhibited, who, at the age of 6, weighed over 205lbs, and The Human Atom, who was actually a 17-month-old baby, 12in high and weighing only 22oz.

In keeping with the mores of the time, none of these entertainments, including the freaks and anatomical exhibitions, were considered to be salacious or unacceptable in any way. In fact, they were regarded as being a completely socially acceptable form of entertainment. Families were welcome and children were particularly encouraged to attend, and Reynolds' Waxworks was promoted as 'an educational exhibition designed to inform, warn, and improve the juvenile personality'.

Reynolds' Waxworks and Exhibition remained very popular throughout the late nineteenth century, and in 1894 curious Liverpudlians could now see 'Princess Paulina, the Living Doll', who was a Dutch dwarf, also known as 'Lady Dot' or the 'Midget Mite'. She stood at a height of just 17in and weighed only 8.5lbs. Sadly, Paulina was only 19 years old when she died in 1895. However, she had been such a popular attraction and quite a celebrity during her lifetime that Reynolds made a waxwork of her, which he displayed for many years afterwards. Visitors could also be amazed by 'Ethnographic attractions featuring a family of genuine Aztecs'!

Determined to use every modern technological development to enhance his exhibitions, Reynolds also displayed a 'Breathing Sleeping Beauty', and an illuminated, sensually sculpted wax figure of 'Ayella, the snake-charming houri'. This model was dressed in a gorgeous and tantalizing oriental costume and draped in writhing model snakes and alligators. She also had electric fittings that lit up the snakes' eyes. On view too was a life-sized, mechanical model of the extremely popular 4ft 6in tall Music Hall comedian and dancer Little Tich (1867–1928), which danced and bowed. Another particularly popular attraction was a fully animated clockwork scene showing an English execution by hanging.

Poster advertising 'the Lion Boy' at Reynolds' Waxworks and Exhibition. (*Discover Liverpool Library*)

Reynolds was particularly anxious to secure a wax model of James Berry (1852–1913), the celebrated and very busy hangman, so he paid this 'master-craftsman' the staggering sum of £100 to sit to have his portrait made in wax. Berry agreed, but Reynolds, who never missed a trick, admitted the public to observe the process, charging them handsomely for the privilege. But the customers got their money's worth too, because during these sessions Mr Hangman Berry regaled people with grisly, detailed descriptions of how some of his 'customers' had gone to their deaths on his gallows!

In 1899 visitors could have seen 'The Wax Head of Jack-The-Ripper, modelled from sketches published in the *Daily Telegraph*, and from witnesses who had actually seen him!', which, considering that no one except the serial killer's slaughtered victims had ever seen him, was quite an achievement!

Amongst other 'freaks' caus-ing a sensation in Liverpool were Millie and Christine

'The Infant Jumbo.'
(*Discover Liverpool Library*)

McKoy (1851–1912), otherwise known as 'Millie-Christine, the Carolina Twins' and also as 'The Two-Headed Nightingale'. Born as black slaves on an American plantation in Carolina, these girls were conjoined twins who sang beautifully, in perfect harmony. Emancipated in 1866, following the end of the American Civil War, they successfully, and happily, toured the world, becoming quite wealthy in the process. When they appeared at the Liverpool Waxworks in 1871 they caused a sensation and Reynolds made a great deal of money from extra ticket sales.

Another of Reynolds' special star-attractions was 'Lionel, the Lion-Headed Boy'. He was advertised as being 'From the forests of Kostroma, Russia, eight years of age and bearing a full and completely natural mane of facial and head hair!' The boy was actually Stefan Bibrowski (1891–1932) from Warsaw. He had been discovered by a German showman who, with the permission of the boy's parents, put him on show around the world. When people saw him in the Lime Street Exhibition they were told that his unfortunate but entirely genuine symptoms had been 'caused by his mother witnessing his father being eaten by a lion'.

One of the first permanent venues in Liverpool to show 'moving pictures', Reynolds' Waxworks and Exhibition survived until 1921, still only charging 3*d* and 6*d* for admission. However, by this time tastes were changing and freak shows were no longer quite as acceptable. The exhibitions were removed and sold, as was the building. In fact, the famous anatomical model collection would quickly reappear, at 29 Paradise Street, as the 'Liverpool Museum of Anatomy'. However, this exhibition admitted adults only and on separate days for each gender! When this museum also closed, in 1937, the collection of disturbing wax body parts was bought by Louis Tussaud's Waxworks in Blackpool. As many people reading this will remember, these were exhibited on the Golden Mile until relatively recently.

The building that once housed the Wax Museum, at No. 12 Lime Street. (*Discover Liverpool Library*)

No. 12 Lime Street reopened in 1922 as Reynolds' Billiard Hall, with a tearoom on the ground floor; by the 1950s it was The Empress Chinese Restaurant. In 1964 the entire block of buildings was demolished and replaced by the new St John's Market. However, and judging by the current popularity of horrific attractions such as The London Dungeon, if Reynolds' Waxworks and Exhibition was to reopen today then I expect it would do a roaring trade!

THE SANCTUARY STONE

The Sanctuary Stone is set in the pavement outside the NatWest Bank on Castle Street in Liverpool and is the oldest surviving medieval relic in the city centre. It has sat here for over eight centuries and is a flat, circular slab of green volcanic rock, about 18in in diameter and with four parallel lines scored across it. The first written reference to the stone appears in 1292, but it is certainly older than this.

The stone was once one of a pair, and its partner stood on Dale Street near the corner of Stanley Street. However, this has long-since vanished and records do not say when or why it was removed. The stones marked the boundaries of the town fairs, which were held annually on 25 July and 11 November and were of vital importance to the developing town.

When King John created his new 'Town and Borough of Leverpul' in 1207, the right to hold a fair was one of the privileges that he granted, and this established Liverpool as a market town as well as an important port and harbour. The fairs brought in a greater range of goods and commodities to the town, as well as merchants, traders and customers from miles around. These people not only traded with each other but they also bought goods and services from the towns-people, which helped to create a burgeoning local economy. However, the reason why the stones had a name other than as simple boundary markers for the market days was because they also signified another privilege granted to the town by the king: the Right of Sanctuary.

For ten days before and after these one-day events protection from arrest was secured within the precincts of the fair, mainly for debtors who would otherwise have been thrown into prison. The Right of

The medieval Sanctuary Stone set into the pavement on Castle Street.
(*Discover Liverpool Library*)

Sanctuary was a temporary guarantee of safety from prosecution that dated from early Anglo-Saxon times. From that period all churches and churchyards in England generally provided refuge for fugitives for forty days, while permanent refuge was available at the great Liberties of Beverley, Durham and Ripon. However, the king regarded Liverpool as being so important that he allowed the town itself this special additional freedom too.

However, this ancient tradition was abolished by Henry VIII, during the Reformation, so it's no use trying to claim 'sanctuary' on Castle Street today!

THE ADELPHI – LIVERPOOL'S 'GRAND HOTEL'

Following the closure of the Ranelagh Pleasure Gardens in Liverpool houses were built on the site. The position of the old White House Tavern was particularly suited, however, for the construction of a new, large luxury hotel. The site was bought by an entrepreneur by the name of James Radley who, in 1826, built and opened the Adelphi Hotel. Standing at the junction of Copperas Hill and Brownlow Hill, overlooking Ranelagh Place, this opulent building provided the highest standards of accommodation and dining. Radley designed it to serve the rapidly developing stagecoach trade, and it quickly became the premier hotel in the town.

With the rapid development of the railways throughout the 1830s and 1840s, and the opening of the main-line terminus station at Lime Street in 1836, there was now a new breed of wealthy traveller. So, to keep pace with their demands for superb accommodation, and to again cater for their wealth and social status, the original hotel was demolished in 1886 and replaced by an entirely new Adelphi Hotel on the same site. That same year the hotel published its own *Adelphi Hotel Guide to Liverpool*, in which it also took the opportunity to prominently advertise its own, even more luxurious facilities.

The Adelphi boasted 300 'well-appointed bedrooms' for which the daily rates ranged from 2s 6d to 6s per night. There were also parlour rooms with adjoining sitting rooms, for which the daily rates ranged from 7s to 21s per night. Additional facilities for guests included a telegraph office, electric lights, an ice house, a billiard room with six tables and a separate banqueting suite.

The table d'hôte dinner, served in the marble-pillared dining room, consisted of 'soup, entree, joint and sweets etc. vegetables and cheese' and cost 6s. One of the most popular and renowned soups served in the hotel, but only from the à la carte menu, was the Adelphi's own turtle soup. Considered a true delicacy, and extremely expensive, hotel chefs prepared this themselves fresh, every day, from their own live turtles!

In the basement of the hotel, in large, specially constructed aquarium tanks, were kept between 150 to 250 edible turtles. These were imported directly to the hotel from the West Indies and the Gulf of Mexico, and then killed and turned into soup in the Adelphi's on-site, purpose-built turtle slaughterhouse! The resulting product was also bottled at the hotel and then sold throughout the country, as well as on the Continent and in the United States, and the Adelphi advertised it particularly as being 'a suitable food for invalids'.

The (second) Adelphi Hotel. (*Courtesy of Liverpool Athenaeum Library*)

In 1892 the hotel was bought by the Midland Railway Company, but by the early years of the twentieth century it was clear to them that, once again, the demands of its clientele had once again outgrown the existing building. So this too was demolished, and in 1914 the company opened what is the current Adelphi Hotel. This quickly became internationally renowned as being one of the most luxurious hotels in Britain, now servicing not only rail passengers but also those wealthy travellers taking trips on the great ocean-going liners; it accommodated them all in opulent surroundings.

The hotel has a large foyer and, at the top of a flight of marble steps, a grand saloon in which, in earlier times, a Palm Court string orchestra would play as guests took afternoon tea. This splendid building was designed by Frank Atkinson, who also designed and decorated the interiors of some of the world's greatest passenger ships and the Selfridges store in London. The Sefton Suite in the hotel is an exact replica of the First Class Smoking Lounge on RMS *Titanic*.

Because of this, the interior of the hotel is often used as a film and television set, especially when scenes are required on board the first-class decks of historic passenger ships. Amongst many other productions, the Adelphi was a location for the 1981 Granada Television production of *Brideshead Revisited*. It was also the location for scenes from the 1997 James Cameron film *Titanic* as well as for *A Night to Remember*, which was an earlier film about the tragedy, produced in 1958.

Some of the world's wealthiest people have stayed at the Adelphi, including royalty and the aristocracy, politicians and famous stars of stage and screen. American president Franklin Roosevelt and his wife, Eleanor, Winston Churchill, Bing Crosby, Charlton Heston, Laurel and Hardy, Frank Sinatra and Judy Garland have all been guests at the hotel.

In 1954 the famous cowboy film star Roy Rogers once rode his equally famous horse, Trigger, up the steps of the hotel, then up its staircases and along its corridors; he then appeared at an upper-front balcony, where they both received the applause and cheers of the crowds standing in the street below. All grand hotels are the scene of such curious incidents, scandals and significant events, and it was whilst he was a guest at the Adelphi, in the early 1970s, that the Russian classical musician Vladimir Ashkenazy announced his defection to the West. However, these were to be the final glory days of the Adelphi as a truly deluxe hotel which catered for the glitterati and intelligentsia of Liverpool and the world.

I have very fond memories of the building, and of its highly professional staff, because as a young man in the late 1960s I would enjoy cocktails with my 'Bohemian' friends in the hotel's outstanding cocktail bar. I would dine out too, in style, in the lavish hotel restaurant and sample with relish the range and quality of its extensive, and expensive, wine list. Sadly, though, and with the almost total decline of Liverpool itself during the 1970s and 1980s, the hotel became neglected and shabby, and its reputation suffered badly.

However, and just as Liverpool fought back to regain its 'world class' status, this too is the ambition of the modern Adelphi. It is a Grade II listed building and, although it remains only a shadow of its former days of elegance and extravagance, it retains all of its original features. The building has 402 bedrooms and these, together with all of its public areas, were refurbished in 2008 at a cost £15 million when Liverpool became the European Capital of Culture. This refurbishment process is continuing, and it is to be hoped that some day the Adelphi Hotel will reclaim its international status as one of Britain's 'Grand Hotels'.

THE HALE DUCK DECOY

One of the most important Scheduled Ancient Monuments in Britain – the duck decoy – can be found just outside the township of Hale.

Lowland coastal areas of England, such as those still around Hale, were not only suitable for pasture in medieval and later times, but the seasonal flooding that takes place in them created marshes and pools that attracted wildfowl to the area. For centuries these birds provided an additional source of food that was important to the local community; such was the case at Hale. Throughout England during the sixteenth and seventeenth centuries, and possibly inspired by the Dutch, an ingenious method of trapping ducks for food and feathers began to become established, and the Hale Duck Decoy is one of the finest surviving examples of this system.

There were 215 duck decoys recorded in 1868, mostly on the east coast of England, but only forty-four of these were working at that time. Today only five such decoys survive – all in nature reserves. However, there were only ever three in the North West, of which Hale is the only survivor. Built in either 1613 or 1631 (historians are unclear), and standing on what is known as 'Decoy Marsh' adjacent to Halegate Farm, the Hale Duck Decoy is a specially constructed, irregular pentagonal pond, surrounded by a wooded copse and a moat that is 16ft wide and crossed by a swing bridge.

The decoy was designed to resemble other, natural coverts that were dotted around the surrounding landscape. These attracted hundreds of waterfowl that annually came to the Hale marshes to nest and breed; and they still do. The ducks were attracted to the decoy because it was secluded and sheltered, and they found the artificially created environment ideal for nesting, believing it to be no different from other nesting sites.

The layout of the duck decoy is particularly ingenious because it is made up of five channels that radiate out from the central pond and which are brick-lined. These are called 'pipes' and are caged over with hoops that are spaced out and covered with netting. They also curve and taper from a wide opening facing onto the pond, into a narrow point deep into the bank. From the air the decoy looks like a large pentagonal star with five curved arms – and is quite special.

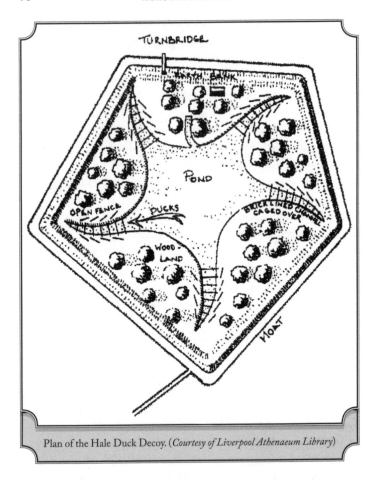

Plan of the Hale Duck Decoy. (*Courtesy of Liverpool Athenaeum Library*)

The mouth of the pipe is a semicircle of about 10–15ft in circumference, so large that it remains unnoticeable from the duck's point of view. This means that the birds swim from the pond into the channels, unaware that they are entering the fat end of a watery wedge. Each pipe is 150ft long and bends out of sight into the woodland, so that the birds do not realise that these lead nowhere, except into suddenly narrowing points with trap-nets at the end.

Between each pipe are small areas of additional woodland, and when the decoy was working, the channels were fenced on both sides, in a zigzag pattern, by slatted screens or closely woven osier fences, 11ft high. These had small holes cut in them at intervals so that a duck hunter could stand concealed behind them at the broad end of the trap and upwind from the nesting birds. Ducks always fly into the wind when taking off, so having five pipes positioned around the pond gave flexibility to the hunter to always set his trap against the wind.

The birds would unwittingly swim into the mouths of the pipes as the hunter watched and waited behind the wooden boards with his special breed of dog. These dynamic little canines were trained to run between the zigzag boards, to draw in the ducks deeper into the trap, and the birds were usually further encouraged to continue down the pipe by the hunter's assistants beating on the fences. The ducks would fly deep into the pipe until they reached the hunter's nets at the end, where they would be easily bagged.

Interestingly, it seems that far from flying away from the dogs, the ducks would fly or swim towards them because they regarded the barking creatures as small predators, and so they wanted to drive them away from their nests in the pond. The dogs used by the hunters were a specific breed, known as Duck Tollers, chosen particularly for their colour. This resembled that of a fox, so would appropriately panic the ducks. The dogs therefore acted as lures as opposed to terriers, and between 750 and 1,500 ducks could be caught each season, making the Hale Duck Decoy a very effective and sophisticated hunting system.

Today the decoy is a haven for ducks, and in the autumn it can attract an average of 800 teal and 400 mallard. In the spring around 100 sheldrake can be found at any given time in the decoy. Although one or two of the pipes, channels, and nets have also been restored, the birds are perfectly safe, as never again will the decoy be used for its original purpose! The surrounding moat has also been cleaned up and de-silted, and its banks renewed and strengthened. Money is also being used to build effective defences against encroachment by an often wild River Mersey.

The Hale Decoy is now open to the public. However, the site is so environmentally sensitive that this can only be accessed on ranger-guided walks and tours, which set off from nearby Pickering's Pasture Nature Reserve. These only take place at certain times of year to limit the impact that visitors have on the decoy. Local rangers are eager to point out that the area surrounding the decoy, Hale Marsh, is treacherous, and they warn people not to attempt to access the decoy unguided or without permission. However, if visitors contact the Ranger Station at Pickering's Pasture then staff are only too happy to pass on information about access. The people who do visit the duck decoy don't regret it!

The Pier Head Floating Landing Stages

Before the middle of the eighteenth century people boarding or leaving ferries and sailing ships using the Port of Liverpool had to do so once the vessels had run up on to the 'Strand'. This was a stretch of open sand and shingle at the bottom of Water Street, which was then at the river's edge, and from which the modern, very busy waterfront roadway of Liverpool takes its name.

Passengers then had to clamber up and down the sides of the vessels using steep, precarious gangplanks or rope ladders. But because so many people were falling into the water, getting injured or simply getting their shoes, feet and legs wet through, something had to be done! So in the 1760s a very narrow, fixed boarding gangway was erected, jutting out into the river from the shoreline in front of St Nicholas's church, which also then stood directly on the riverbank. This new jetty was known as the 'North Pier' and gave this part of Liverpool's waterfront its modern name – the Pier Head. However, when George's Dock was built, in 1771, the jetty was pulled down. Ferry passengers then had to get ashore via dangerous, narrow steps that had been cut into the riverside wall of the new dock. The Three Graces, Royal Liver, Cunard and Port of Liverpool buildings now stand over the site of the former George's Dock.

By the mid-nineteenth century ferry traffic was increasing substantially, so a safer and more appropriate method of embarkation and disembarkation was needed. Also, there were ever greater numbers of travellers getting off and on great ships that were sailing to and from the four corners of the world. And so in 1847 the first floating wooden landing stage was built at the Pier Head at a cost of £60,000.

This was over 500ft long and 80ft wide and was named George's Landing Stage after the dock. The stage was supported on thirty-nine iron buoyancy pontoons, each one 80ft long, 10ft wide and 6ft deep. These could be entered for inspection and maintenance via manholes in the deck surface.

Even so, this great quay was soon not long enough and, in 1873, the George's Stage was extended with the addition of a new and even longer floating platform. Also largely constructed of timber this was named Princes Landing Stage after the nearby Princes Dock, which had opened in 1821. However, the opening ceremony for this had hardly been planned when, on 28 July 1874, the new wooden quay was swept by a catastrophic fire that completely destroyed it.

Remarkably, and after only two years, the great structure was completely rebuilt at a cost of £370,000, and 'the like of which is not to be found at any other port in the world'. The combined landing stages, known locally as 'The Pier Head Landing Stage', floated on the river on 200 huge pontoons. It was anchored to the land by a series of solid metal connectors, great chains and covered gangways, which allowed it to rise and fall with the tides.

White Star's SS *Baltic* at the Landing Stage, Liverpool. (*The History Press*)

The landing stages provided docking facilities for the large numbers of Mersey ferry boats that once sailed to eleven destinations on the Wirral; for passenger ships, then regularly visiting the Isle of Man and Llandudno; for other passenger and goods vessels; and, eventually, for the great transatlantic liners. At the time of its construction, and for many years afterwards, this was the world's longest floating structure and it stretched for almost half a mile from Mann Island to Princes Dock. A guidebook of 1904 described it as having 'Refreshment Rooms, Retiring Rooms, Telegraph and Telephone Offices, and every convenience for passengers.'

In fact, this wonderful range of buildings, also mostly constructed from wood, included shops, covered waiting areas, lavatories, cafés, a post office, administration offices and shelters for the dockhands and boatmen. Both landing stages also housed a remarkable complex of services and structures. There were bell towers; sophisticated, adjustable fingerpost signs, indicating at which point along the stage the various ferry boats were docking; and two-tier drawbridge gangplanks, allowing passengers to get on and off both the upper and lower decks of the ferries.

The Pier Head Landing Stage fire, 28 July 1874.
(*Courtesy of Liverpool Athenaeum Library*)

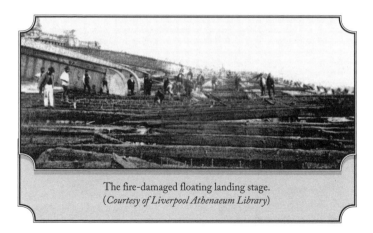

The fire-damaged floating landing stage.
(*Courtesy of Liverpool Athenaeum Library*)

The George's Landing Stage in 1904.
(*Courtesy of Liverpool Athenaeum Library*)

The Prince's Landing Stage in 1904.
(*Courtesy of Liverpool Athenaeum Library*)

The full landing stage was also wide enough to take cars, lorries and heavy goods wagons, which would drive onto the stage down a remarkable floating iron roadway. This formed a fixed link between the stage and the land and was composed of a series of great metal plates, hinged together horizontally. This design allowed the roadway to respond to the movement of the waves and to rise and fall with the landing stage at the ebb and flow of the tides. The floating roadway was demolished in the 1980s. But in 2007 it was redesigned and reconstructed as a single-span road bridge to service the new Cruise Liner Terminal.

The Pier Head Landing Stage was always a bustle of thriving activity and commerce, with a hubbub of chatter and noise that washed over and around it, just as the River Mersey itself could wash over and around it when the weather was stormy or the tide was high! As a child I was fascinated by the way the whole structure undulated with the movement of the river waves and by how the buildings all along its length, which were connected to each other with overlaps and flexible joints, would move with it. All this accompanied by the creaks and groans of the old woodwork.

Whenever the weather was especially rough the ferry boats could come in with a great, hard 'thump' against the rubber-tyre and woven-rope buffers. This would then drive the whole landing stage sharply backwards, occasionally knocking people off their feet as a result. This was great fun all round – at least for us kids!

As I write this, I recall the sound of the waves, the creaking of the landing stage, the roaring of the great diesel engines of the boats, the jostling of the crowds of passengers, the shouts of the men as they caught the ropes to tie up the vessels, the cries of the seagulls wheeling overhead and the salty smell of the great river.

I remember too the thrill of watching the ferry boats coming and going, and admiring the skill with which their captains guided them safely into dock against the jetty, whatever the weather conditions. And I miss it, because, sadly, this wonderful, exciting, evocative example of Victorian engineering ingenuity was demolished in the early 1970s. The great wooden floating landing stage was replaced by a much shorter, and staggeringly arid, concrete and steel structure. This has now been replaced, within the last few years, with a structure that is only marginally better!

Even so, and despite this small flaw, the excitement and glamour of the Pier Head has now returned to Liverpool, as the waterfront has seen major investment over the last decade. The central river frontage has also been restored, redesigned and re-established as a major hub of commerce, community and entertainment – a world-class waterfront for a world-class port.

The Legend of the Eagle and Child

The Earls of Derby, whose family seat is at Knowsley, just to the east of Liverpool, are descended from Adam de Aldithley (Stanley), born in around 1005. His descendant, the slightly impoverished Sir John Stanley (1350–1414), married Isabel de Lathom (1355–1414) in 1385. Isabel was a descendant of the founder of the de Lathom dynasty, Robert de Lathom (*d.*1199), and her family were exceptionally wealthy indeed.

The de Lathoms held the very large estate at Knowsley, with a sizeable hunting lodge at its heart that would eventually become today's

Knowsley Hall. They also owned an exceptionally larger estate, and a palace at Lathom near Ormskirk. Indeed, Isabel's family had been prominent in south Lancashire for many generations.

Nevertheless, neither Sir John nor his new bride could expect to inherit great wealth from their families because they both had so many relatives taking precedence. Nevertheless, by 1390 fate had removed these obstacles from Isabel's path, and she – and therefore her husband – gained possession of valuable properties and vast, rich acres of land all over what were then Lancashire and Cheshire. These included estates on the Wirral Peninsula, especially around Bidston, where the family built Bidston Hall. In fact, by the time of their deaths (both in 1414 and by natural causes), their holdings of land and property had become even more considerable.

The motto of the Stanley family, the Earls of Derby, is *Sans Changer*, which translates as 'Without Change'. Their emblem depicts a large eagle with its wings spread open above a baby in a basket, although this crest originally belonged to the de Lathom family. There are a number of tales that explain how this image came to be adopted by the family, but the most popular is that of the foundling child.

This story tells how Sir Thomas Lathom (*d*.1382), Isabel's father, had desperately wanted a male heir but only had his one daughter. Sir Thomas's wife, Joan de Ferrers, was getting older and he believed that there was no hope. So he found a compliant woman of quality and together they produced Thomas's much-longed-for son. Even so, how could this otherwise illegitimate child be introduced convincingly into the family and be accepted by them so that he could someday inherit the Lathom titles and property? Sir Thomas had an idea.

He arranged for a servant to take the infant and place it at the foot of a tree in Tarlescough Woods, which was a wild section of his Lathom estate. Sir Thomas knew that in the high branches of this tree was an eagle's nest. Then, taking his wife past the tree on the pretext of going for a walk, the couple found the baby boy as if by accident. Lady Joan was convinced that the eagle had snatched the baby and dropped it and that now, by a miracle, the child had been saved from death. Lady Joan asked Sir Thomas if they could adopt the child as their heir. Naturally, Thomas agreed. The Christian name Oskatel, which had been his true mother's name, was given to

Knowsley Hall. (*The History Press*)

the foundling, and he was brought up as a legitimate member of the de Lathom family.

The story goes on to relate how, as he neared death and beset by guilt, Sir Thomas confessed all and bequeathed the bulk of his estate to his daughter, Isabel. To his own, adopted but illegitimate son, Thomas now left only the manors of Irlam and Urmston, near Manchester, and some lands in Cheshire. Oskatel de Lathom, later knighted by the king, retired to his Cheshire estates and founded the family of Lathom of Astbury. So perhaps the story has more than a grain of truth in it?

As we have seen, Isabel did indeed inherit a vast fortune from her father, who actually had two perfectly legitimate sons, both born after his daughter. The first he named Thomas after himself, and the second he named Edward, so his subterfuge, true or not, would have proved to have been unnecessary. Whatever the origins of the legend may actually be, the Eagle and Child was adopted as the de Lathom family crest. This romantic tale too has been handed down through generations of Stanleys and, like the Eagle and Child crest, is now fully embedded in the legends and heritage of the Earls of Derby.

FIRE IN THE MENAGERIE

As the stories in this book are confirming, the people of Liverpool and Merseyside have always enjoyed thrilling and unusual entertainments, but they especially liked zoos. Between the early 1800s and the late 1930s there were at least six of them in Liverpool alone! These all had to be supplied, though, with a wide range of creatures that were exciting and novel enough to entertain and satisfy the demanding tastes of the paying public. Fortunately for the zoos and the people, in the whole field of animal trading few men were more significant and able than Liverpool-born William Cross (1840–1900).

Already a renowned animal importer, from around 1879 Cross established a new major base of operations at Cross's Menagerie and Museum, located in a large warehouse at the corner of Rigby and Earle Streets in Liverpool. This was near to St Paul's Square, which is now at the heart of the city's modern commercial district. Cross based his business here because it was close to the docks and to the ships that brought in, and exported again, his live wild animals, birds and reptiles.

Cross was one of the most important and successful importers of animals, and he supplied these to zoological gardens and private collections all over Britain, Europe and around the world. He employed his own hunters in the more far-flung countries, so always ensured a ready supply of some of the most exotic creatures. He also advertised extensively and had agents operating all over the globe.

So successful was his business that Cross decided to open up his vast warehouse to the paying public, including its hundreds of cages and compounds, and he made a great deal of money as a result! This was because he was a showman at heart, who certainly knew how to appeal to the Scousers' passion for the thrilling, the bizarre and the extraordinary.

He exhibited a wide range of creatures from his premises, such as bison, giraffes and rhinos, which most people marvelled at because they had only ever read about them or seen them in pictures. But thousands of people were also drawn to his great menagerie to witness exhibitions of apparently fearless men wrestling with lions and to learn how to ride zebras. They could also gaze in wonder at that rarest of specimens, advertised as 'a white elephant from Siam', although rumour had it that Cross simply painted an ordinary elephant with at least fifty coats of a mixture of whitewash and plaster of paris!

However, on 25 August 1898 there was a serious fire at Cross's Menagerie. Reporting this disaster a newspaper stated:

> The terrible-scene in the early hours of yesterday cannot be imagined, except by one who has seen a prairie fire or a jungle conflagration. The collection of animals at this place is one of the most remarkable in any civilized country, and it is constantly changing … The caged beasts themselves gave the alarm, their keen smell detecting the fire at the first outbreak, and when the flames took hold of the building their screams and roars of terror must have been appalling.
>
> The poor brutes were mostly suffocated, for you cannot deal with lions and tigers as you would with horses, and open the doors and let them out. Either the cages must be moved bodily or the occupants abandoned, and the fire took such rapid hold that there was no time for heroic measures. The loss in lions, tigers, and leopards was considerable; all being burned to death; but a baby elephant, it is interesting to know, escaped unharmed.

The great clouds of smoke were so blinding and suffocating that all attempts at rescue were beaten back. Among the creatures that either choked or burned to death were four lions, five leopards, a Bengal tiger, a jaguar, an adult puma, a black opossum, twenty-eight prairie marmots and a crested eagle hawk. Also killed were a vulture, two hyenas, three cheetahs, a peccary, four rare foxes, two Virginian owls, two very rare northern China owls and two eagles.

During the inspection of the building, after the fire had finally been extinguished, the full tragedy began to be revealed. Most of the animals had been seared beyond recognition in the blaze, their limbs in many cases being burnt entirely away. It was also clear that one of the lions had made a frantic effort to escape before being overcome. The remains of its forepaws were found protruding through the bars of its cage, against which its head was pressed with obvious force and, as the newspaper described, 'showing the frantic strength which he must have used in his last mighty effort to escape the flames'.

Cross's Menagerie in 1901.
(*Discover Liverpool Library*)

However, some animals were found to be still alive, if barely. These included three hyenas, although each was severely burned about the head. One was so injured and in such agonised distress that it was decided to kill it. When the cage door was opened the demented creature began biting everyone and everything around it. The animal immediately bolted through the door, but one keeper managed to leap on it and pin it down by its hind legs. This enabled the speedy intervention of two other keepers, who quickly put a noose around its neck and throttled it, finally putting it out of its agonised misery. However, four cassowaries, a black bear and a kangaroo were rescued, terrified and soaking wet from the fire-hoses but otherwise completely unharmed.

Inside a typical Victorian circus. (*LOC, LC-USZ62-24554*)

Quite a number of animals had managed to escape the building during the fire, not just the baby elephant. These wreaked havoc in the surrounding streets before all being eventually recaptured, luckily without injury to themselves or to members of the public. Just as fortunately, the menagerie was fully insured and so was completely rebuilt and restocked. Within a year or so it was 'business as usual', and in the 1902 edition of the *Stranger in Liverpool*, a popular and thoroughly detailed tourist guide to the city, a report stated:

> Cross's menagerie is situated at the corner of Rigby Street, off Old Hall Street (which is reached by crossing the Exchange Flags behind the Town Hall) and within a stone's throw of the Exchange Station, is this depot, undoubtedly one of the most complete trading menageries in the world …
>
> Beasts, birds, reptiles, and other representatives of the lower creation are dealt with, and so varied is the business that the proprietor boasts of his readiness to supply, on the shortest notice, anything with life in it from a humming bird to an elephant.

> The menagerie is open to the public daily from 10.00am to 5.00pm, at a charge of 6d. per head, and, as many of the magnificent animals are constantly going through a course of training, a visit to the establishment will prove both interesting and instructive.

After William Cross retired the business was then managed by his sons, William Simpson Cross (1873–1920) and James Conrad Cross (1879–1952). It is not clear when Cross's Menagerie closed, but it was certainly still operating in 1911. William Junior now had overall responsibility for the business, and during the 1900s he expanded the family's interests by renting the former mansion house and riverside estate of slave-trader and railway pioneer John Moss (1782–1858) at Otterspool in south Liverpool.

Here, in around 1914, he opened a new zoo. Amongst its attractions were a toothless, clawless, one-eyed lion, and an entirely bald-headed, bad-tempered badger. These animals, together with llamas, a buffalo and many others from his collection, were allowed to wander freely around the grounds and amongst the paying public: there was no Health and Safety Executive in those days you see! This zoo closed in 1925 when Liverpool Corporation bought the Otterspool estate to convert it into the public parkland that is now known as Otterspool Park and Promenade.

There are no longer any zoos or menageries in Liverpool, the nearest now being at Chester Zoo, and the triumphs and tragedies of William Cross and his sons are now only a memory. However, there is a thrilling safari park at Knowsley to the east of the city, on the estate of the 19th Earl of Derby; there Merseysiders' continuing passion for exciting animals can still find satisfaction in the twenty-first century.

A poster advertising Cross's Menagerie, from 1901. (*Courtesy of Liverpool Athenaeum Library*)

MOLLY BUSHELL AND HER EVERTON TOFFEE SHOP

Each of the suburbs of modern Liverpool was once a village or township in its own right. Most of these are listed in William the Conqueror's Domesday Book of 1086 and many pre-date the now great city by many centuries.

One of the earliest of these communities, Everton, was originally a significant rural township standing high on the eastern ridge above Liverpool. Little now remains of ancient Everton Village, except the old village lock-up, standing in what remains of the village green, and two of the original streets, named Village Street and Browside, which once ran through its heart. All of the village's homes and houses have long since been demolished and replaced by the modern, expansive, landscaped Everton Park. These included a thatched cottage that had been built here around 1690 and which overlooked the village green.

This was the home of a local woman by the name of Molly Bushell (1746–1818) and, from 1753, it was here that she began to make the boiled sweets that she called Everton Toffee. The recipe was not Molly's own but had been given to her by its inventor, Doctor James Gerrard, who was a local physician and town councillor in Liverpool. Molly made her toffee in an open oven at the rear of her home, and it quickly became very popular.

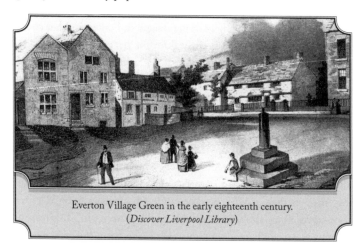

Everton Village Green in the early eighteenth century.
(*Discover Liverpool Library*)

The cottage in which Molly began her business stood near to an older and already famous cottage. In 1644 this had been commandeered by Prince Rupert of the Rhine, the nephew of King Charles I (1600–49). He had used this as his headquarters whilst he besieged Liverpool Town during the English Civil War. By the time Molly began selling her toffee Prince Rupert's Cottage had already become a tourist attraction in the village, bringing curious sightseers to Everton from miles around. They would visit the famous building, drink in the local taverns, and picnic on the green with its spectacular views across the Wirral to Wales and the Irish Sea. Now they could also buy Molly Bushell's increasingly renowned toffee and make a real day out!

During the time that Molly lived by the historic cottage, its current occupiers decided to sell off some of the furniture. At the sale, Molly bought the chair that was claimed to have supported the royal bottom of Rupert. Now, as well as bolstering her own buttocks, Molly used this curious piece of furniture to provide her with a profitable sideline to her toffee sales. She now charged her customers a few extra pennies to see and to sit on the significant wooden chair.

Over the years the toffee became much prized, not just by local people but also by the wealthier classes in the area. And so in 1783 Molly moved across the green into a larger house, standing on Village Street. Here she converted the lower part of her home into a shop and began to expand her product range.

In the beginning, and for twenty years, Molly had worked alone but now she enlisted the help of her daughter, Esther, and her cousin, Mrs Sarah Cooper. Business thrived for the next thirty years. In due course, Everton Toffee became a great favourite with Queen Victoria and her family, who had batches of it regularly shipped to Windsor Castle. Charles Dickens also ordered regular supplies of the sweet.

As Everton began to expand, the centre of life in the village was around the village green and Molly's toffee shop, and the number of 'tourists' now coming to the village began to rise significantly. These people now became souvenir hunters who pulled chunks out from the walls of Prince Rupert's Cottage. Eventually, there were so many day-trippers that, in 1787, it was considered necessary to build a local lock-up 'to house drunks and unruly revellers overnight'. This became a well-known landmark, sometimes called 'The Stone Jug', and it is one of only two surviving village gaols in Liverpool, the other being located in the middle of Wavertree Village to the south of the city.

When Molly Bushell died in 1818 her recipe, and her goods and chattels, including Prince Rupert's chair, now passed to her cousin Sarah Cooper, so stayed in the family. Mrs Cooper continued to make and sell the celebrated and still popular Everton Toffee from new premises on Browside. However, the depredations of the tourists continued to weaken the structure of Prince Rupert's Cottage and, in 1845, it had to be pulled down. The previous year, and for

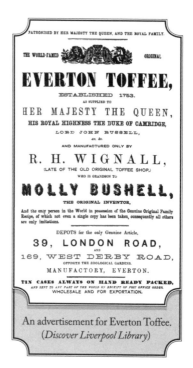

An advertisement for Everton Toffee.
(*Discover Liverpool Library*)

similar reasons, Molly Bushell's original cottage and toffee shop had already been demolished. Sometime around 1884 the Browside Toffee Shop was also demolished, as was the rest of the street.

Nevertheless, the family had by this time acquired another property and shop at No. 1 Netherfield Road, which was still in the heart of Everton Village. Everton Toffee continued to be sold by them from this address until the late nineteenth century, when the last of the toffee-making dynasty, Clara Bannister, retired. This shop and the toffee recipe were subsequently bought by the confectionary firm Nobletts in 1894. They now used the trademark 'Mother Noblett', based on an image of Molly Bushell, to sell their version of Everton Toffee.

Nobletts was eventually sold to the famous firm of Barker & Dobson, who first put the distinctive stripes on the individual sweets. This company was eventually bought out by the Taveners sweet company, who continue to sell Everton Toffee. Nevertheless, this company

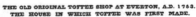

THE OLD ORIGINAL TOFFEE SHOP AT EVERTON, A.D. 1753.
THE HOUSE IN WHICH TOFFEE WAS FIRST MADE.

PATRONISED BY HER MAJESTY THE QUEEN, AND THE ROYAL FAMILY.

THE WORLD-FAMED ORIGINAL

EVERTON TOFFEE,

ESTABLISHED 1753,

AS SUPPLIED TO

HER MAJESTY THE QUEEN

An advertisement for Everton Toffee, showing the Village Street toffee shop.
(*Discover Liverpool Library*)

do not claim that their recipe is authentic, so don't assume that the humbugs you now eat when you buy modern Everton Toffees taste the same as the ones that Molly Bushell's customers would have known!

The Netherfield Road Toffee Shop was also eventually pulled down to make way for new housing, but the Everton lock-up still stands and is now a listed building. It is in excellent condition and well maintained by Liverpool City Council. Everton Football Club took the image of the lock-up as the central device on its club emblem, and the club's nickname remains 'The Toffees' after Molly Bushell's famous toffee. In fact, at the start of every home game the 'Toffee Lady' comes onto the pitch. Dressed in eighteenth-century garb she carries a wicker basket. This latter-day Molly Bushell takes Everton Toffees from her basket and scatters them into the crowds. At the end of the game she comes out again, and if Everton FC has lost the match, she weeps; if, however, they have won, she dances a jig!

Interestingly, descendants of Molly Bushell now live at Neston, across the River Mersey on the Wirral Peninsula, and they still own Molly's original copper toffee-making pan and Prince Rupert's wooden chair.

THE FIRST MERSEY TUNNEL?

Most people know that there are two road tunnels under the River Mersey. The first of these was begun in 1925 and eventually opened by King George V (1865–1936) and Queen Mary (1867–1953) in July 1934. Running between Liverpool and Birkenhead, this was named 'Queensway', and when it was built it was the longest underwater road tunnel in the world at almost 2.25 miles (3.62 kilometres) long. It cost £7,723,000 to construct.

In 1967 work began on the second Mersey road tunnel, running between Liverpool and Wallasey. This was opened on 24 June 1971 by Her Majesty the Queen (b.1926). It was named Kingsway by her, in tribute to her father, King George VI (1895–1952). Predating both of these, though, is an underwater rail tunnel. This was opened in 1886, with trains first running underground from Central to James Street stations in Liverpool and then continuing beneath the Mersey to Hamilton Square Station in Birkenhead. The first passenger trains using this tunnel were steam locomotives; the line was not electrified until 1903.

However, apart from inspection tunnels for these, and for certain utilities, it is now believed that there is a very much older tunnel beneath the waters of the Mersey. This was excavated entirely by hand for the use of pedestrians and perhaps pack animals!

For around 300 years, until the Reformation in the early sixteenth century, much of what was then south Lancashire was the property of the Cistercian Order of Monks. This Christian community had their principal monastery at Whalley Abbey near Clitheroe and a settlement at Stanlawe on the Wirral Peninsula, in what was then Cheshire. This was where the Stanlow Oil Refinery now stands, and having become well established in this district, in 1178 the order built an abbey here. However, near their abbey they only had access to limited arable land, the quality of which was quite poor.

Medieval monks. (*The History Press*)

At this time the River Mersey teemed with fish and the land on the Liverpool side was particularly rich, fertile and well irrigated by freshwater streams. To provision their local religious community and generate income, the Cistercians wanted to take advantage of this. But first they needed permission to do so.

In 1264 they approached Adam of Garston, the lord of the manor of what are now the Liverpool districts of Garston, Aigburth and Speke, which still border the river. From his seat at the now long-demolished Aigburth Hall, Adam agreed to allow the Cistercians to farm on his estates. The monks began to breed pigs at Speke and to grow cereals and other crops in the Garston and Aigburth areas, where they built granaries. For many years during the Middle Ages the Cistercians held extensive fisheries in Garston, specialising in flat fish and shrimps, which were sold in nearby Liverpool Town and in the surrounding villages.

They also operated a number of watermills, which were fed by a stream that has its source in Allerton. This stream still runs to the river under modern Garston, through a culvert that was specially constructed in the nineteenth century as the village expanded and began to become industrialised.

However, the only surviving evidence that the Cistercians were once in south Liverpool is Stanlawe Grange. This stands at No. 2 Aigburth Hall Drive in Grassendale. They built this sometime around 1290 as a large, cruck-frame barn for the storage of livestock and produce. It also had accommodation space for three or four monks. Eventually becoming a farmhouse, in the later decades of the twentieth century the building was sympathetically restored and converted into two adjoining private houses. Despite these many changes, the 'Grange' remains the oldest continuously occupied structure within the Liverpool city boundary.

To get across from one side of the river to the other, the Stanlawe monks had to sail or row across the often turbulent waters of the Mersey. However, local legends say that to enable them to still work their mills and farm their lands at Liverpool when the river was too wild to navigate, the monks built a tunnel under the river. This directly connected their Lancashire holdings to their monastery on the Wirral. To create this they excavated and extended natural caverns and openings beneath the Mersey. The tales of their tunnel may indeed have some basis in fact. This is because the Wirral, just like Liverpool, is riddled with underground passageways and caves, many of which are natural but many more man-made.

On what must have been a twisting and rugged route, lit only by tallow lamps or candles that they would have carried with them, the monks made their way to their swine fields at Spic (now Speke), their fish farms at Gaerstun (Garston) and their farmlands at Ackeberth (Aigburth). That these holdings existed near ancient Liverpool is certain, and we know the Cistercians were rowing across the river before and during the time that the Benedictines operated their ferry to Liverpool from Woodside at modern Birkenhead from the early twelfth century.

In 1279 Stanlawe Abbey was flooded and damaged, in 1286 its tower fell down and in 1289 it was ruined by fire. This was too much for the monks, who now moved back to their main house at Whalley. By 1294 there were only five monks and the abbot left at Stanlawe, with one residing at the Grange at Aigburth. They finally left the area in 1538 during the Dissolution of the Monasteries in the reign of King Henry VIII.

Although both sides of the river have now been heavily built over, the entrances to this legendary tunnel have been located at both Stanlow and at Garston. Nevertheless, these are securely sealed and disguised to deter any would-be explorers. We shall just have to wait to discover if chance, accident or archaeological determination either prove or disprove the legends of the first Mersey tunnel.

PROPAGANDA AGAINST PROSTITUTION – A QUESTIONABLE DETERRENT

In 1827 large copies of a striking poster began to appear on the outsides of buildings in Liverpool, especially taverns, warehouses and docksides in the more unsavoury sections of the port that were known as 'Sailortown'. This caught the attention of passers-by with a particularly striking heading, set out as follows:

Full and Particular account of the Shocking and

AWFUL DEATH

of Twelve Young Women

Who were Smothered on Monday last, Sept. 3rd 1827, in the Infirmary, being afflicted with an incurable Malady which they caught of [*sic*] some sailors.

This was an attempt by the authorities and the Church of the day to terrify young women in particular about what might happen to them if they fell into prostitution. This was an increasing problem in the port at the beginning of the nineteenth century, as the increasing population and the lack of available work were forcing ordinary people to find other ways of eking out a living. Crime was the alternative for men and prostitution the alternative for women and girls.

The illustration used in the 1827 propaganda poster, showing the young prostitutes being smothered. (*Courtesy of Liverpool Athenaeum Library*)

Many desperate young women were being forced, by the poverty of their circumstances or by the brutal desperation of their fathers or husbands, to sell their bodies on the streets and wharves of the town. In typical Victorian fashion, there was no attempt to address the social issues that were creating young prostitutes, but considerable effort was made to threaten and to punish those who 'strayed from the path of righteous and seemly behaviour'.

Below the headline on the poster was a vivid woodcut image. This clearly showed twelve young women being smothered to death under a massive quilt or mattress. They were being 'put out of their misery' by three, large, well-dressed, uniformed men who were clearly officials of some sort. Underneath the picture was some text and a narrative poem describing the circumstances of the young girls' plight and the reasons why they had been brought to such a grisly end. I reproduce this below in full, together with the illustration:

A Grecian ship arrived in this port in the month of August last, having about thirty hands on board, when no sooner had the vessel come into the river Mersey, than a number of unfortunate young women went on board to barter both body and soul for a trifling sum of money.

It is the nature of sin to carry along with it its own punishment, and the awful denunciation of God's displeasure not unfrequently commences in this, and terminates in the terrors of another World.

For the foreigners communicated a disease of such an infectious and dreadful nature that it baffled the united skill of the most eminent and experienced of the faculty of Liverpool, and proved too stubborn for any antidote that could be applied in this country.

After every means had been used, without producing the desired effect, the symptoms of this dreadful malady became more and more alarming.

The flesh first turned yellow, then became spongy like a honey comb, and afterwards became black, and began to drop off their bones in large lumps. So offensive was the stench that arose from the putrid state of their bodies that no person, however desirous, could approach their beds or give them any relief.

On Saturday, another consultation of the medical gentlemen connected with the infirmary was held, when, after a most laborious and length-ened conference, they came to the awful question that these wretched young women should be smothered with nitre and sulphur, the easiest and most effectual method of putting a stop to the raging infection.

These unfortunate women's names are,

Jane Williams, aged 18; Mary Frame, aged 16; Elizabeth Watts, aged 15; Mary Evans, aged 20; Margaret Jones, aged 17: Sarah Rich, aged 17; Catherine Howell, aged 17; Elizabeth Bennett, aged 16: Anna Loyd, aged 19; Ellen Harper, aged 17; Sarah Jones, aged 18; and Lydia Neads, aged 16.

Lament, lament, the woeful fate of twelve young females dear,
Who suffered such a death of late, most painful for to hear.

And let all those young females know, who stray from virtues ways,
That Vice did prove their overthrow, and shortened their days

A foreign ship in port arrived, of thirty hands or so,
And twelve gay damsels young and blythe, straightway on board did go.

And there a loathsome, vile disease, infectious and foul,
Did on these twelve young women seize, and raged without control.

The flesh did rot upon their bones, spungy, like honeycomb;
Their dismal, cries, their sighs and moans, would pierc'd a heart of stone.

The doctors to their pain and grief, beheld their suff'rings great,
But could afford them no relief, the plague for to abate.

All human means being tried in vain, but could not mend the case,
To put the sufferers out of pain, an awful scene took place.

The dread infection to destroy, which through the town might spread,
Their precious lives were sacrificed, they smothered were in bed.

Now ponder well this dismal scene, young women all I pray;
Twelve blooming girls of seventeen have thus been swept away.

And left their parents sore to weep, and friends who loved them dear,
Tho' sin and vice your hearts entice, the sting is most severe.

Of course, this incident never actually took place, it was simply a contrived 'horror story' purporting to be the truth. Whether or not this had the desired effect is not recorded, but that is highly unlikely. As long as there were women in dire straits and desperation, and men equally desperate to buy the only commodity these unfortunate women had available, prostitution in Liverpool, and everywhere else in the world, continued to flourish.

THE POISONER, THE LANDLADY AND THE BROOCH

In 1907 in the Assembly Rooms in Albion Street, New Brighton, a public lecture was given by a visiting homeopathic doctor. He was married to a woman named Cora Turner (1873–1910), who was a mediocre theatrical singer popularly known by her stage name of Belle Elmore. Belle was in her early 30s and was originally from New York, where she had met her husband. The couple moved to England and settled in London.

Belle was known to be overbearing and a nag, who was fond of collecting diamonds and pink, frilly clothes. She also liked a drink and flirting with men. Belle quite relentlessly nagged and bullied her husband, often in public, which he just seemed to submit to. The doctor was a small and very mild-mannered man with a high, bald forehead, a thick moustache and rather bulbous eyes. He wore gold-rimmed spectacles and always dressed smartly, if very conservatively.

Fed up with his domineering wife's treatment of him, the doctor turned his attentions to other women, particularly to his 28-year-old secretary, Ethel Clara le Neve (1883–1967). However, Belle discovered this and threatened to leave him penniless. Despite her mediocre talent she was actually earning good money and held the household accounts.

Belle Elmore.
(*LOC, LC-DIG-ggbain-05164*)

Three years after her husband's New Brighton lecture, Belle disappeared. Soon afterwards the doctor moved his girlfriend, Ethel, into the family home. Before long she was seen to be wearing Belle Elmore's clothes and jewellery, and, in fact, it was largely due to a Liverpool pub landlady that the hunt for the missing music hall entertainer began.

Mary Egerton (after whom the modern 'Ma Egerton's Stage Door' pub in Liverpool is named) was also a renowned theatrical agent and a personal friend of Belle Elmore. On one of her many trips to London from Liverpool early in 1910 Mary happened to see Belle's husband out walking with an attractive young woman on his arm. The Liverpool landlady noticed that the girl was wearing a distinctive 'starburst' brooch, which she recognised as belonging to her friend. Belle called this her 'Rising Sun', and it was a gorgeous pendant, whose black centre-stone was cut with a cluster of diamonds. From this extended a ray-beam design of inlaid smaller diamonds.

As Belle had, by this time, been missing for some time, Mary Egerton reported her suspicions to the police.

The Crippen family home in Camden, as pictured in 1910.
(*Courtesy of Ma Egerton's Stage Door, Liverpool*)

Ma Egerton (standing, third from the right) in the 1920s.
(*Courtesy of Ma Egerton's Stage Door, Liverpool*)

Ma Egerton in the 1960s.
(*Courtesy of Ma Egerton's Stage Door, Liverpool*)

Scotland Yard detectives now questioned the doctor about his missing wife. He told them that she had left him for another man, moved to America and then unexpectedly died. However, his feeble explanation increased the suspicions of the police, who continued their investigations.

One day, whilst only the doctor's maid was in the house, a detective from Scotland Yard, Chief Inspector Dew, visited his home to see if he could find any trace of the missing woman or any evidence of foul play. He scoured the building from top to bottom and discovered (buried under the floor of the coal cellar and wrapped in a pair of men's pyjamas, according to reports) 'a compact mass of animal remains which, on expert investigation, proved to be the greatest part of the contents of a human body …'

There was no head, all the limbs were missing and there were no bones, except for what appeared to be part of a human thigh. The remains were declared to be female and were found to contain the toxic compound hyoscine hydrobromide. It was this drug that was now believed to have caused the death of the headless, limbless victim, and it was proved that the doctor had actually bought some of this.

In the meantime, and using the name of 'Robinson', the doctor had panicked and fled overseas, first to Holland. From here, he boarded the SS *Montrose* bound for Canada. With him went Ethel, but disguised as his young son. A warrant was issued by the Metropolitan Police for the arrest of Belle Elmore's husband and Miss Ethel le Neve. An international alarm, together with very detailed descriptions, was sent out across Europe requesting any information about the fugitives.

Henry Kendall, the captain of the *Montrose*, whilst reading a newspaper in his cabin, saw a report about what had now been dubbed 'The London Cellar Murder' and the wanted pair. He became suspicious of two of his passengers, especially as he had seen the 'apparent' males affectionately holding hands. He immediately sent the world's first wireless telegraph message used to track fugitives, which read:

> Have strong suspicion that the London Cellar Murderer and accomplice are amongst saloon passengers.
> Moustache shaved off, growing a beard.
> Accomplice dressed as a boy, voice, manner, and build; undoubtedly a girl.

As soon as this message was received at Scotland Yard, Chief Inspector Dew boarded a faster ship, the SS *Laurentic*, on 31 July 1910, and he was waiting at the quayside when the *Montrose* arrived in Canada. As soon as the doctor and Ethel stepped from the ship onto the dockside they were immediately arrested. The pair were brought straight back to Britain, sailing to Liverpool, from where they were taken to London. Here, the diffident medic stood trial for his wife's murder. Four days after his trial was concluded, his lover was tried separately.

Of course, the one-time New Brighton lecturer was none other than Dr Hawley Harvey Crippen, MD (*b*.1862). Even though he claimed he had bought the drug for one of his homeopathic remedies, the jury took only twenty-seven minutes to reach their verdict, and he was found guilty of the murder of his wife. Crippen was hanged at Pentonville Prison on 23 November 1910, and he asked that a photograph of Ethel be buried with him. His request was granted. Ethel le Neve, however, was acquitted of complicity in the murder and released.

Crippen and Ethel le Neve on trial. (*LOC, LC-DIG-ggbain-08612*)

Adopting the travelling name of 'Miss Allen', on the morning that Crippen was being hanged Ethel le Neve sailed for New York and then travelled on to Toronto. Ethel changed her surname once again, calling herself 'Harvey' in acknowledgement of her lover's middle name. Sometime during the First World War (1914–18) Ethel returned to London where she married a clerk by the name of Stanley Smith. They had a number of children, and Ethel died in 1967, at the age of 84.

After the trial and Crippen's execution, Belle Elmore's brooch, together with the rest of her jewels and much of her clothing and other possessions, was auctioned off. Charles Fry, a pawnbroker in Wallasey, bought the brooch and put it on display in the window of his shop at No. 242 Liscard Road. What has since happened to the jewel no one is quite sure! However, had it not been for that brooch, and the Liverpool pub landlady who recognised it, the murderer of Belle Elmore (Cora Crippen) might never have been discovered or brought to justice.

PROJECT REDSAND AND THE MERSEY FORTS

Soon after the outbreak of the Second World War, in September 1939, an English civil engineer named Guy Maunsell (1884–1961) had an ingenious idea for a particular type of offshore defence system. Although regarded by some as mad, nevertheless his final plans were taken seriously by the War Office. He went on to design free-standing, linked, fortified towers to be anchored on the seabed in vulnerable waters around Britain.

Men and munitions could be stationed on these 'forts', mines could be laid from them, and they could spot enemy ships or aircraft approaching and then launch attacks against them. So Project Redsand was established, and four forts were manufactured and installed in the estuary of the River Thames.

These proved to be so successful that, early in 1941, the Admiralty asked Maunsell to design a special series of defensive forts for the estuary of the River Mersey. This was now considered to be a priority project because the North Atlantic Convoys of fleets of merchant navy supply ships from Canada and the British Empire, and from the United States, were sailing regularly into the Port of Liverpool.

The Mersey Forts. (*Courtesy of Liverpool Athenaeum Library*)

After the fall of France to the Nazis in June 1940, and until America came into the war in December 1941, Britain stood virtually alone against Hitler's occupied 'Fortress Europa'. The convoys were vital to our country's survival, bringing supplies of fuel, food, medicines, munitions and machinery to beleaguered Britain.

Hitler attacked these convoys relentlessly with warships, aircraft and, especially, fleets of U-boats. These patrolled the Atlantic Ocean, the Irish Sea, Liverpool Bay and the estuary of the River Mersey. This made the defence of the river, and the docklands of Wallasey, Birkenhead and, of course, Liverpool, an absolute necessity.

This great naval action became known as the Battle of the Atlantic, and it was the longest, continual action of the entire conflict. This is because it began the day war broke out, in 1939, and only ended with the final surrender of Germany in May 1945.

Developing his original concept, Maunsell designed each of his new defensive units for Liverpool to consist of four hollow reinforced-concrete legs, each 50ft high and 3ft in diameter, and mounted on a huge, lozenge-shaped concrete base. These legs supported a rectangular steel 'house', 36ft long on each side and with two levels. Military equipment and armaments were housed on the upper level, and a garrison of men lived and operated from the lower floor. Each fort comprised seven such units, linked together by tubular steel catwalks over the sea.

Three of these fort complexes were towed out into Liverpool Bay and anchored on the seabed, and each one accommodated up to 265 men! The Mersey Forts were arranged in three batteries in the Mersey estuary 16 miles down channel from New Brighton. They were located at three points: Queen's Fort near the Bar Lightship, the Burbo Fort south of this and the Formby Fort anchored north of the Bar.

The River Thames Forts shot down twenty-two planes and thirty flying bombs and were instrumental in the loss of one U-boat, which was scuttled after coming under fire from Tongue Sands Fort. However, the Mersey Forts never fired a shot!

Nevertheless, they were a deterrent, and they successfully acted as forward observation points and communications centres, which were vital to the Battle of the Atlantic. After the war, demolition of the Mersey Forts began in the early 1950s and was completed in 1955.

There were other defensive devices set up for the protection of wartime Merseyside, including electrically-fired mines that were placed underwater on the riverbed between New Brighton and Gladstone Dock. These were controlled from an on-shore observation post. There were also torpedo tubes that were placed on New Brighton Landing Stage, and from which missiles could be fired, to travel on or below the surface of the river.

Although subjected to catastrophic bombing raids, which resulted in severe damage and much loss of life and serious injury, the role that Liverpool and the rest of Merseyside played in the defence of Britain, and in the assault on Hitler's military, airborne, and naval might, cannot be underestimated.

Project Redsand and the Mersey Forts may not have fired a shot in anger, but they certainly played their own part in the wartime story of the Mersey and in our ultimate victory against the obscenity that is Fascism.

WHISKY GALORE!

Overlooking the churchyard of Our Lady and St Nicholas's church, off Chapel Street in Liverpool, stands the grand office building named Mersey Chambers. This is renowned for the white Liver Bird that stands on its pediment and for the fact that it was once the headquarters of the Harrison Shipping Line.

Perhaps the most famous vessel in the company's fleet was SS *Politician*. This was an 8,000-ton cargo ship which sailed from Liverpool on 3 February 1941, at the height of the Second World War. She was bound for Kingston, Jamaica, and New Orleans, and she was carrying a cargo that included 28,000 cases of malt whisky.

However, on 5 February 1941 the large cargo vessel encountered gale-force winds off the coast of the Outer Hebrides in Scotland. Unable to maintain control, the ship was driven onto the rocks and shoals of the Island of Eriskay, where she ran aground. The *Politician* was at risk of sinking, so her crew abandoned her, but they all managed to make it safely to the island, where they were looked after by the local community, unharmed.

The former head office of the Harrison Shipping Line,
complete with the white Liver Bird above the pediment.
(*Discover Liverpool Library*)

Despite the storm, which soon abated, the *Politician* did not sink, and when the locals discovered what was onboard, they hatched a plan. Their own supplies of whisky had all been used up because of wartime rationing, so they were determined to recover as many cases of spirits as they could before these were swallowed up by the waves rather than by them. It was obvious to the islanders that Customs and Excise officials would soon arrive to attempt to remove the ship's valuable and tempting cargo, so the men organised a series of rapid, completely illegal nighttime raids on the stranded vessel.

Word of the alcoholic treasure trove had spread very quickly by this time to the other Hebridean islands, and soon boats were coming from as far away as Lewis to join in the unofficial 'salvage' operation. The highly motivated Scotsmen executed their mission with superb organisation and stealthy efficiency. In all, they relieved *Politician* of something like 24,000 bottles of whisky before the customs officers eventually arrived.

Nevertheless, the resident customs officer on Eriskay, Charles McColl, was enraged by what the local people had done, and he pressured somewhat reluctant island police officers into searching for the stolen whisky. Communities were raided and cottages and crofts ransacked in the searches, but almost none of the bottles were found. The ingenuity of the islanders meant that the whisky had been skillfully hidden or disguised, or they had simply quickly drunk it rather than lose it to the authorities.

Soon official attempts were indeed carried out to salvage *Politician*'s cargo, but these were not at all successful. Before long permission was given for the ship, and its remaining contents, to be blown up. To the great dismay of the islanders, what they regarded as a wanton act of criminal insanity was carried out by the Royal Navy, and the Hebridean people grieved long and bitterly over the waste of such a vast quantity of 'liquid gold'.

In 1947 the renowned author Sir Compton MacKenzie published an entertaining novel based on this incident. In 1949 this was used as the story for an equally entertaining and now famous film, produced by the Ealing Film Studios. Both the book and the film were entitled *Whisky Galore!*

THE VAMPIRES' BURIALS

For centuries, from Medieval times until the mid-nineteenth century, in towns and villages across Britain, it was usual to bury executed criminals and suicides in unconsecrated ground. It was also quite common that such people would be deliberately buried at crossroads on the outskirts of communities. This was because of the prevalent superstition that such people might return from the dead to terrorise the living or to take revenge on their accusers.

Many people also believed that if such people did rise from their graves they would do so as vampires. These resurrected, undead predators would then attack their victims and drink their blood whilst also sucking their souls from their soon to be lifeless bodies, perhaps then condemning these innocents to also walk the Earth as vampires.

There were a number of reasons why crossroads were chosen as burial sites, particularly for the most brutal of murderers or vicious of criminals, the main one being the symbolism of the Christian cross, as represented by the intersecting roads or tracks. It was believed that this would permanently trap any restless spirits underground. It was also assumed that if a corpse did manage to dig its way up to the surface again, it would be confused by the four roads and so be less likely to find its way back to its intended victims.

Such irrational beliefs were just as common in and around Liverpool as anywhere else, and especially in what were then more remote local communities. Such was the case in Everton when, sometime around 1680, such a burial took place at a crossroads known as Four Lane Ends. This appears to have been located in the vicinity of St George's church, on what was to become Kelper Street, which is now part of Everton Park.

It was here that a local man was buried after he had brutally murdered his wife and then committed suicide in a bout of guilt. Not only was he interred at the ancient crossroads but his body was impaled through the heart with a great spike. This was to keep him pinned to the ground once he had been covered over with earth. It is said that his body still lies there because, even in subsequent rebuildings of the district, no one was prepared to exhume and relocate a body that might then reanimate from the dead.

Another such interment was carried out not far from this Everton burial. This took place sometime in the eighteenth century, when a man was executed and buried after he had bitten his wife in the neck and then drunk her blood until she died of exsanguination. This burial was carried out at the junction of Rupert Lane (which also lies under modern Everton Park), Breck Road, Heyworth Street and Everton Road, which all still exist, as does the crossroads.

The tale is still told locally of how this 'Everton Vampire' did indeed return from the dead, despite his crossroads burial. He would rise in the middle of the night to terrorise and attack women. His blood-thirsty rampages were only stopped when his grave was opened, his body turned face down and a wooden stake driven deep into his heart through his back. After this he was not seen again, but it is said that his corpse too still lies uneasily beneath the modern road junction.

Burying a suspected vampire at the crossroads at midnight.
(*Discover Liverpool Library*)

Burying such individuals at crossroads did not end until 1825, when an Act of Parliament made the practice illegal. Even so, evidence of such burials began to be, quite literally, unearthed during the great expansion of Liverpool during the mid-nineteenth century. This was a time when densely packed new streets and houses were being laid out in previously outlying districts of the town.

In 1854 sewer pipes were first being laid along Tithebarn Street, which is one of the original seven streets of Liverpool. Sewers were also being laid in the roads leading off this ancient thoroughfare, so trenches for these were being excavated across this entire area.

When the workmen began excavating at the crossroads junction of Tithebarn Street with Hatton Garden, Great Crosshall Street and Vauxhall Road, to their horror they found the rotting remains of a male corpse. They were not surprised, however, and accepted the reasonableness of such a burial. This was confirmed in their minds, as well as those of the public, when inquiries revealed that this was the corpse of Thomas Cosgrove.

A number of local people remembered how, nearly forty years previously, in 1815, Cosgrove had murdered his wife at their home in nearby Cheapside and had then poisoned himself. Because he was a suicide and a murderer Cosgrove had been buried at the crossroads, probably at midnight. Once again, it was expected that he too would now spend eternity at the centre of a cross and so be forever trapped below ground and unable to return as another undead predator.

As well as driving stakes through the bodies of such people, sometimes their heads would be severed as an added precaution against resurrection, but records do not say if this was the case with Cosgrove. What they do say is that he was simply reburied in the same place. Does this mean that there is yet another potential vampire still lying under the tarmac of one of Liverpool's road junctions? If so, how many more such corpses lie buried beneath the busy city streets?

Within Way and the Old Ford

The deadly Hale Ford claimed many a victim …
(*Shutterstock, 178139033*)

Immediately to the right of the Manor House, at the heart of the township of Hale, is a road named Within Way. This narrow lane leads south, after a mile or so, down to the banks of the River Mersey. The name 'within' seems to derive from 'withy' or 'with', which was an ancient term to describe osier twigs cut from a species of willow tree. These long, thin, strong but pliable sticks were woven into baskets or fences. They were also used to produce large lattice frames or 'wattles' that then formed the walls of buildings. A paste mixture of mud and clay called 'daub', which was often combined with cow or horse manure, was then spread onto the wattles. This meant that osier twigs were a vital raw material for many centuries.

The name given to Within Way probably indicates that the lane once wended its way through plantations of these willows. What remains a narrow track still leads to the only place where, in ancient times and when Hale was still part of Lancashire, a ferry rowed across to Runcorn on the Cheshire side of the river. But sometime during the reign of King John this had been 'discontinued for want of a boat'. From this time the ferry moved further upstream to operate between Widnes and Runcorn, and the only way to now cross the river from Hale was either on foot or on horseback.

Of course, this could only be accomplished at very low tide, which was still a treacherous undertaking because of the quicksands, shifting sandbanks and sudden rush of deep, incoming tides. Before industrialisation, of course, the river was much wider than it is now, by a considerable margin, which will give some idea of the risks involved in attempting to ford it. Over the centuries many people, and even more animals, have met their deaths crossing the notorious Hale Ford. Gravestones in the burial ground of Hale parish church tell tales of people drowning in the Mersey. A few of their bodies were recovered, whilst others were lost forever in the shifting sands, deep channels and swirling fogs of the Mersey, which is why some of these graves are actually empty.

In 1423 a certain John Walley tried to ride across from Hale to his home in Runcorn. With him he had two horses laden with fish from Formby. Tragically, he was caught by the turbulent inrush of the tide, and he drowned in the attempt, although both his horses, complete with their cargo, made it safely across.

During the Civil War (1642–49) troops from both sides of the conflict, often with prisoners, made occasional crossings at the Hale Ford. Again, not everyone managed to safely avoid the tide or negotiate the deceptive shallows and dangerous sands. This was especially the case for those unfortunate captives who had their hands tied or who had been bound to their fellows.

Crossings of the river on foot continued right up to the end of the nineteenth century, when work began on the construction of the Manchester Ship Canal in November 1882. This then cut off all horse and foot access to the other side of the river. Even so, there are records of horses and carts being driven across as late as 1880. Indeed, the last time that it appears to have been crossed was just before excavation work began on the new waterway, when an intrepid (or foolhardy) man decided to ford the river on foot in both directions, 'just to see if this could still be accomplished'! He made it from Hale to what is now Weston Point, with the river sloshing about his ankles. However, on the return trip the water was clearly beginning to rise, but he remained undaunted. Indeed, he removed all of his clothes and completed the hazardous crossing with them held above his head to keep them dry and with the River Mersey lapping about his neck and shoulders!

If you wish to retrace the route in general down Within Way, at least as far as the riverbank (I would not recommend that you walk any further!), then do take a ramble down the narrow lane which is closed to vehicles. Not only will the walk itself be very pleasant (weather permitting of course) but the views will be rewarding too.

A DICTATOR COMES TO LIVERPOOL

Corporal Adolf Hitler.
(*Discover Liverpool Library*)

It is clearly the case that Liverpool has always been home to many wonderful people and to quite a number of eccentric characters as well. Sadly, the city has also had its share of some quite unsavoury people. However, the worst of these residents may well have been the twentieth century's greatest villain, Adolf Hitler.

The father of the German Dictator was named Alois Schicklgruber (1837–1903), but believing this surname was preventing him from advancing in his career as a middle-ranking clerk in the Austrian Customs Service, in 1876 Alois changed his family name to 'Heidler'. However, another clerk, this time in the Registrar's Department, inaccurately wrote the name down as 'Hitler' in the official records, and so it remained.

Alois, who was a notorious womaniser, married three times, the last time to Klara Poelzl (1860–1907). They had six children, one of whom, born on 20 April 1889, was Adolf. The family had moved to the important Austrian town of Linz in 1894, and this was where the boy was to spend most of his childhood.

Adolf Hitler was a sickly child who was doted on by his rather ineffectual mother. She was completely dominated by her husband, who had no interest in his children and spent most of his time in the beerkeller or keeping his many hives of honeybees. By the time Adolf reached his late teens he had grown into a moody, irritable, anti-social and permanently dishevelled young man. Adolf's miserable and angst-ridden personality seems to have been largely innate, but his negative temperament was certainly exacerbated by his many disagreements with his overbearing and bullying father. If Alois communicated with his children at all it was mostly to persistently yell at them.

Records of Hitler's early life are limited because, once he became the 'German Fuehrer', he had most of them destroyed or rewritten. What documents do survive confirm that his mother died of breast cancer in 1907, with a grief-stricken Adolf at her bedside. Records then show that by 1908 Adolf Hitler had moved to Vienna. He had set up home here to study, in the hope of fulfilling his ambition of becoming a great architect and painter. However, young Hitler simply was not talented enough and was refused a place at the Viennese Academy of Fine Arts. This rejection added to his resentments, as did the fact that he then had to take a series of menial jobs in the Austrian capital, simply to keep from starving.

There are a number of telling gaps in Hitler's personal history, particularly between the years of 1912 and 1914. It is now generally accepted that he was about to be called up for national service in the military, something he really did not want to do; it is likely that he simply ran away. Many people now believe that, in fact, in November 1912, and at the age of 23, Adolf Hitler left Vienna and travelled to England.

At least, this is what a typewritten manuscript seems to say. This set of papers is alleged to have been written sometime in the 1930s by Hitler's sister-in-law, Bridget Hitler (1891–1969), and it was discovered in the New York Public Library in 1972. Signed by Bridget, and entitled *My Brother-in-Law Adolf* (Ref. No. ZL–344), the accuracy of the neatly bound pages is questioned by some but completely accepted by others. In the text is confirmation of a long-held belief that Adolf Hitler spent some of his 'missing years' in the Toxteth district of Liverpool.

By the time of Adolf Hitler's disappearance from Vienna, his half-brother, Alois Hitler Junior (1882–1956), had already left the family home, in 1896, at the age of 14. Also failing to find a meaningful career, he resorted to theft and served two prison terms, one in 1900 and another in 1902, as a result. Spending some time in Paris, with equally unsuccessful results, Alois eventually came to London where he found work as a cook. In 1908 he moved to Dublin where, at a horse show in 1909, he met 17-year-old Bridget Dowling.

Bridgid Hitler, and her son William, on their lecture tour in pre-war America. (*Discover Liverpool Library*)

The couple had ambitions, so they eloped to the 'city of opportunity', Liverpool. Here they ran a small restaurant in Dale Street, a small hotel on Mount Pleasant and a boarding house on Parliament Street. However, each of these business ventures was unsuccessful, so the Hitlers of Liverpool had very little money. Alois Junior and Bridget rented a flat at No. 102 Upper Stanhope Street, which runs off Princes Road in Toxteth. It was here, on 12 March 1911, that their only child, William Patrick Hitler, was born.

His half-brother, Alois Jnr.
(*Discover Liverpool Library*)

In her manuscript, Bridget Hitler describes how her half-brother-in-law, Adolf, came to stay with them at Stanhope Street between November 1912 and April 1913. However, his miserable and bitter nature, as well as his general untidiness and limited level of personal hygiene, meant that he was an irritating and unwelcome guest, at least as far as Bridget was concerned.

She describes how Adolf would mope about and that when she insisted that he get out from under her feet and find some work, he simply wandered the streets of the great city. There is no evidence that Adolf Hitler ever took any form of work during his short time in Liverpool, but during the 1970s, when I was employed in Toxteth as a community worker, I met a number of older local people who remembered him. They confirmed (or perhaps simply repeated) many of the myths and legends surrounding Hitler in Liverpool.

They said how he was a solitary figure, drinking silently in the corners of pubs in Toxteth, as well as in the Poste House pub in Cumberland Street in the city centre. They told me too how he also spent a lot of time in the Walker Art Gallery in William Brown Street. This stands adjacent to the tall commemorative column dedicated to the Duke of Wellington.

It seems that before going into the gallery Hitler would stand gazing up at the figure of the 'Iron Duke', then, inside the Walker, he would stare intently at the large portrait of 'Napoleon crossing the Alps'. This undeniably impressive picture dominates the left-hand staircase leading up from the ground floor and hangs today where it did during Hitler's alleged visits. Perhaps the powerful life-stories of these two great military leaders fuelled Adolf Hitler's own militaristic ambitions for world domination.

It is also said that he spent hours at Liverpool's docksides, watching the hundreds of ships coming into and out of what was one of the world's busiest ports. Perhaps this 'inside knowledge' of Britain's maritime supremacy and Liverpool's strategic importance is the reason why, during the Second World War, he was so determined to bomb the port and city into oblivion. Perhaps, too, this is why he launched his relentless U-boat attacks against British naval convoys in and around Liverpool Bay during what became known as the Battle of the Atlantic.

Whatever is the case, and however he spent his time in Liverpool, by April 1913 he had outstayed his welcome. His half-brother bought Adolf a railway ticket back to Germany, put him on a train at Lime Street railway station and the young man returned to his homeland.

Here, and at the outbreak of the First World War in July 1914, he found himself serving as a dispatch runner on the Western Front in France and Belgium. He was promoted to the rank of corporal and was wounded at the Battle of the Somme in October 1916. Again, records are unclear, but the wound seems to have been relatively serious and was in his groin or thigh area. Whatever the specifics of this injury actually were, this led to the popular belief that he had lost a testicle as a result. This gave rise to the poignant little ditty that was sung by Allied soldiers throughout the war, to the tune of 'Colonel Bogey', and the opening line of which is 'Hitler has only got one ball ...'!

Whilst much of this story so far may be apocryphal, the rest, however, is history.

In 1942 Adolf Hitler stated firmly that he had no family, declaring 'I belong only to my people.' But the eventual discovery of Bridget Hitler's manuscript by the English historian Robert Payne (1911–83) seemed to throw new light on this, especially when Payne wrote *The Life and Death of Adolf Hitler* in 1973. This book is what the Liverpool author Beryl Bainbridge (1932–2010) used as a basis for her 1978 novel *Young Adolf*. In this story she develops Bridget Hitler's narrative to tell her own tale of the miserable young Austrian's time in the city.

The marriage between Alois Hitler Junior and Bridget Dowling was not a happy one. Alois seems to have shared some family traits and was violent towards his wife and child. He returned to Germany but Bridget refused to go with him, staying in Liverpool with her son. In 1924 Alois contracted a bigamous marriage in Germany, although Bridget agreed not to prosecute him as he promised to support her and William – which he never did!

Records say that by 1934 Alois Hitler was a right-wing politician running a restaurant in Berlin. It also seems that William visited Germany a number of times in the early 1930s but his uncle, now the Führer, refused to acknowledge or support him. Equally, it seems that Hitler and his half-brother were never close. The respected historian Professor Sir Ian Kershaw states:

> Adolf Hitler never really had a great deal of time for him. During the Third Reich when Adolf Hitler had reached the pinnacle of power, Alois had very little to do with him. Afterwards he changed his name and lived in obscurity and died, I think Hamburg, in 1956. So, no evidence of a close relationship between the two men.

After his failure to gain his uncle's patronage, William Hitler returned to his mother in England from where, as the war began to loom, they moved to America.

Here, in 1939, Hitler's nephew went on a lecture tour of the USA, accompanied by his mother. He also wrote a sensationalist book entitled *What the German People are Really Thinking*. He applied for and was granted American citizenship, and in 1944 he joined the American Navy. Here he saw active service, fighting against the forces of his uncle.

When he was discharged from the navy in 1947, William Hitler changed his name to William Patrick Stewart-Houston. He went on to marry a German girl named Phyllis, and they set up home in Long Island, New York. Before William died, in 1987, he and his wife had four sons: Alex (*b*.1949–), Louis (*b*.1951–), Howard (1957–89) and Brian (*b*.1965–). There is a wholly unsubstantiated story that his three surviving sons, who still live in New York, have made a private agreement not to marry or have children in order to help the Hitler name die out.

A former editor of the *Liverpool Echo* newspaper, Mike Unger, has written an excellent book on this story, *The Hitlers of Liverpool*, which is recommended to those who want to further explore this peculiar but plausible story. However, there is a final and ironic twist to this tale.

During the war Liverpool was the most heavily bombed city in Britain, outside London, and all of Merseyside was subjected to saturation bombing by the German Luftwaffe. The final air raid on the city took place on 10 January 1942, and amongst the houses damaged were a number of properties on Upper Stanhope Street, including No. 102! The site was eventually cleared of debris, and all that now remains of the house where Adolf Hitler may (or may not) have stayed in Liverpool is a rather pleasant square of open grass, set in an ordinary housing estate in Toxteth.

The Moreton Hovercraft

A hovercraft, or ACV (Air Cushion Vehicle), is a passenger or cargo vessel that can travel over land, water, ice or mud, as its name indicates, by floating on a cushion of air. This is drawn down at force through a powerful fan-driven air-suction vent on the roof of the craft. This air is then blasted out from beneath its rubber-skirted base, creating lift, and forward movement is provided by rear- or side-mounted propulsion fans.

In 1962 the concrete embankment that forms part of the sea-defences at the foot of Leasowe Lighthouse was the site of the world's first hovercraft service. This was scheduled to run, on an experimental basis, between Moreton Shore on the Wirral and Rhyl on the North Wales coast from 20 July to 16 September.

THE WORLD'S FIRST HOVERCOACH
THE VICKERS VA-3 OPERATED BY BRITISH UNITED AIRWAYS ON B P FUELS AND OILS

The Moreton to Rhyl Hovercraft. (*Discover Liverpool Library*)

Operated by British United Airways, the Vickers VA–3 was a very noisy vehicle that was officially known as a Hover Coach. It was state of the art for the time and even fitted with the latest ship-to-shore radio telephones. These provided direct communication links between the craft and both Moreton and Rhyl. It also had its own sophisticated closed-circuit TV system on board so that the captain and crew could see inside the hovercraft's cabin as well as getting a clear view of what was behind the vessel. This equipment was supplied and fitted by the Pye Telecommunications Group Ltd, an organisation with which I have no connection!

The hovercraft was expected to make twelve crossings a day. However, the service operators succeeded in doing this on only six days during the short lifetime of the service. On another four days they managed ten trips a day. The rest of the time the number of crossings varied and, in fact, the hovercraft ran on only nineteen of the total number of days that the service was supposed to run. This was because of high winds or rough seas, which frequently made the crossing impossible, although one of its two engines was always cutting out as well!

The final hovercraft trip was made on Friday, 14 September 1962. The vessel left Moreton at 1.15 p.m., but halfway across one of its two engines failed again. The other soon followed, and it barely made it to the Welsh seaside resort. The weather the following day was so bad that repairs could not be made, and the next day, Sunday, 16 September, the hovercraft broke free from its moorings with its captain on board. This intrepid seaman, Captain Old, managed to get the engine going and stopped the hovercraft drifting out to sea.

When the tide went out he managed to beach his vessel on the Rhyl shore, but the following day the weather worsened considerably and the hovercraft broke free again. The three men who happened to be on board at the time, including Captain Old, could not stop it being blown out to sea again and could not start the engines. They radioed for the Rhyl Lifeboat, which took them off the dead vessel a quarter of a mile out to sea, leaving the hovercraft to its fate on the turbulent seas. Fortunately, the wind was so strong, and blowing in the right direction, that the abandoned hovercraft was driven back to shore, crashing into the promenade wall at Rhyl.

Here, and in appalling weather conditions, people eventually managed to secure it, even though it was being repeatedly pounded against the sea wall by the wind and the waves. Two mobile cranes were brought in to hoist the stricken vessel out of the water, and at 7.30 a.m. on the morning of Monday, 17 September 1962 the bold attempt to establish a Moreton to Rhyl hovercraft service came to a sad end. Nevertheless, the hovercraft was an amazing technological and engineering achievement, and it always drew great crowds of thrilled and excited spectators – amongst them, as an 11-year-old boy, myself.

People came from miles around to watch the Hover Coach arrive and take off, and my young friends and I particularly loved the roaring racket it used to make. On a number of occasions we were especially excited to watch seagulls flying above the vessel, hoping that they would get so close to the great air intake that they would be sucked down into the mechanism. This happened quite a lot, and we would cheer when the unfortunate birds emerged again, this time being spray-blasted out from underneath the great rubber skirt of the hovercraft as a cloud of blood-stained feathers – but then small boys are amused by such things!

Doctor Solomon and the Balm of Gilead

Sometime between 1791 and 1796 a failed boot-polish and hair curler salesman came to Liverpool to seek his fortune. Whatever his original name might have been, by the time he arrived in the town he was calling himself 'Doctor Samuel Solomon'. Born around 1769, his credentials for such a title was a medical degree that he had he bought from Edinburgh University.

Doctor Samuel Solomon.
(*Courtesy of Liverpool Athenaeum Library*)

Recognising that anyone professing medical expertise would be very likely to become successful and wealthy in the rapidly growing, and extremely overcrowded town, he set up his consulting rooms in Marybone, just off Tithebarn Street. However, trade was surprisingly slow. He was not attracting as many patients as he had expected, so needed something to boost his income. This is when he had the idea of creating his own patent medicine.

Using an innate sense of what would sell, and a clear gift for marketing, Samuel produced and bottled a very tasty, warming, invigorating tonic, which he called 'Doctor Samuel Solomon's Cordial Balm of Gilead'. The name of his product itself was enough to inspire confidence, but so too was his advertising. He distributed leaflets and put up posters all over the town and, for those who could not read, held free public meetings. These were always overcrowded with eager people excited to hear for themselves about this wonderful new miracle medicine that, apparently, cured everything!

His leaflets boldly stated:

Cordial Balm of Gilead is a sure and certain remedy for all nature of afflictions, to wit,

Ague and the rheumatics;

Fever of the senses, and the vapours;

Constipation and discomfort in the bowels;

Excessive production of bodily wastes;

Aches in the head and confusion of the vision;

General malaise;

Lowness of spirits;

Scrofula and related ills;

All natures of venereal affliction;

All form of female afflictions;

Incapacity of the male member;

Priapism; and

Onanism – that destructive habit of a private nature.

So there was something for everyone here! At his meetings he became one of the first entrepreneurs to promote a product using 'the satisfied customer'. Solomon paid people to stand on the platform and enthusiastically attest to the undoubted efficacy of the Balm of Gilead. One such beneficiary of the good doctor's miracle cure boldly declared, to a rapt and enthusiastic audience:

For six years I was afflicted with a nervous disorder; but, hearing of your famous Cordial Balm of Gilead, I hath given it a fair trial. The symptoms of my disorder were that I oftentimes found my head heavy, with my vision strangely uncertain, and an odd sensation in my forehead … All liquors disagreed with my stomach … except porter or a little brandy and water.

I was also frequently troubled with a continual belching and hiccupping; oftentimes for weeks together, which hath lasted for these three years past. And, to add to my afflictions, I frequently suffered from a great passing of wind from my other bodily orifice; that caused much discomfort and annoyance to my family and associates.

However, the wondrous benefit of three bottles of your Cordial Balm of Gilead hath so removed my disorders that I now wish to purchase a five-pound case.

It was cheaper to buy a case of twelve bottles for £5 than it was to buy single bottles, which cost half a guinea each. This was an incredibly high amount to charge and yet despite, or perhaps because of, the price, he sold bottles of his remedy in prodigious amounts. Working on the assumption that 'if it's expensive then it must be good' – a mistake that we often still make today – people were only too willing to pay his asking price. And they kept coming back for more and more and more!

Hardly a ship left the port without cases of Balm of Gilead for the crew or passengers, or for their captains to sell overseas. Indeed, such was the reputation of the medicine, and of the amazingly charismatic Samuel Solomon, that he soon had 400 agencies selling his product across Britain, sixteen in America and others around the world. Samuel very quickly became one of Britain's wealthiest men.

In fact, he had so much money that he built two grand mansions for himself and his family, as he had now married and had three daughters. One of these homes, which he named Gilead House, stood on a landscaped estate that covered much of the modern district of Fairfield in Liverpool. He also built Mossley Hill House on another large estate, this time to the south of the town. He also drove around in a handsome carriage drawn by four pure white stallions, acknowledging the greetings and the respect afforded to him by citizens of every rank.

On his estate at Mossley Hill, and so that he could be as grand in death as he was in life, Solomon built a large mausoleum. This was a spectacular and highly ornate structure. Built in gleaming, and very expensive, pure white sandstone, the mausoleum had several doors and was surmounted by a small, conical obelisk that was surrounded by four cone-shaped pinnacles. It was ornamented all over with statuary, carvings and many other adornments, and it was described as being a miniature version of one of the Wonders of the World!

Solomon died in 1819 and was interred in his mausoleum, together with some members of his family. But this is not where the story ends.

In 1840 Mossley Hill House, and Solomon's mausoleum, were bought by the London and North Western Railway Company, who wanted to build an extension to their railway line across the former private estate. Both structures were pulled down but not before all the bodies were removed from the great tomb and reburied in the great necropolis at Low Hill. This is now an area of plain parkland known as

Grant Gardens, which stands at the corner of Everton Road and West Derby Road. However, the bodies of Samuel Solomon and his family, together with the corpses of over 80,000 people, still lie there, under the grass where people picnic, play football and walk their dogs!

In 1846 Gilead House in Fairfield was also pulled down, to make way for streets of terraced houses to accommodate the rapidly increasing number of working-class families that were moving into the district. What was once Solomon's great estate now lies between Farnworth Street and Sheil Road, and under twenty-one streets, including, naturally, Solomon, Balm and Gilead Streets!

But why was Solomon so successful? Why did he sell so many bottles of his Cordial Balm of Gilead? Did it work? Did it really cure all of those ailments? Of course not! People certainly fell prey to his salesmanship and advertising skills, but they clearly kept taking the medicine and buying it in quantity. It was only after the 'doctor' had died that his closely guarded secret recipe was finally revealed.

Samuel Solomon's quack remedy was simply an infusion of cardamom seeds, lemon peel, tincture of cantharides (Spanish fly), Sicilian oregano and Demerara sugar, steeped in a solution of 10 per cent water and 90 per cent fine French brandy! Solomon also recommended that his cordial be mixed with wine before drinking, which clearly means that his customers and patients were so drunk, if not heavily sedated, that they did not care what they were otherwise suffering from. This is also why they kept coming back for more!

For a few years after Solomon's death a little rhyme did the rounds of the streets and taverns of the town; it ran:

Great Solomon has gone,
His home and sepulchre and Balm,
If his mixture did mankind no good,
At least it did no harm.

The Man in the Iron Coffin

As we have seen, during the Second World War Merseyside suffered massive aerial bombardment by the Germans, and Liverpool city

One of Liverpool's many urban bomb craters; inside one was found
a 'man in the iron coffin'. (*Discover Liverpool Library*)

centre in particular was devastated. Bombed buildings and craters
pockmarked Liverpool and its suburbs, and it was in 1943 that a bomb
blast created such a deep crater that the explosion revealed something
that had lain long buried. At the corner of Great Homer Street and
Fulford Road a rusting iron cylinder had been exposed.

This was just over 6ft long and around 2ft wide, and seemingly completely sealed at both ends. Because the authorities had more pressing
matters to deal with other than this curiosity – war was still raging and
Hitler was determined to bomb Liverpool into oblivion – the cylinder
was simply left where it lay.

The strange object became a play-place for local children and a temporary seat for weary passers-by, and gypsies used it as a workbench on
which to make artificial flowers to sell around the surviving streets and
houses. The cylinder became so familiar that no one seemed to give
much thought to it, until a few years later.

Curiously, it was on Friday, 13 July 1945 that some local children were playing 'tick' and 'hide-and-seek' around the bomb crater. These provided playgrounds for children, including myself, well into the 1950s and '60s. Hiding from his playmates behind the large metal cylinder, a 9-year-old boy named Tommy Lawless noticed something poking out of the end of it. Taking a closer look, he discovered that the cylinder had opened up at one end and that a boot was now sticking out.

Calling to his mates, their game was soon replaced by shared fascination as Tommy took hold of the boot and pulled. To his surprise it came away quite easily, but, and to the shock of all the children, it revealed a human leg and foot bones. Fighting their natural instinct to further explore their macabre discovery, the boys simply stood guard over it whilst Tommy ran off to find the local constable.

A few minutes later the boy returned with a bobbie on the beat – who were then much more numerous than they are today – who took charge of the now even more intriguing object. He arranged for its immediate removal to the city mortuary.

The cylinder was now subjected to the first real examination since it had first been uncovered by the bomb blast, and it was seen to be a piece of sheet iron that had been formed into a cylinder and then riveted together. There was a lid at one end, which had also been riveted in place. The other end had been pressed together, rather like the end of a tube of toothpaste, but for some reason this had now come apart to reveal its grisly contents. When the tube was cut open an immaculately dressed male body, in an advanced state of decomposition, was found inside.

The clothes seemed to be of nineteenth-century origin in that the cadaver was wearing a frock coat; narrow, striped trousers; a thin bow tie; and his boots were clearly of Victorian design.

The man had been lying, at full stretch, on some form of hessian cloth or sacking, with his head resting on a brick. The pathologists laid his body on the mortuary slab to begin a thorough examination and to see if a cause of death could be established. It could not. However, what they did discover only added to the mystery.

Firstly, it was confirmed that the body was of a male who had been middle-aged and in reasonable health, judging by the condition of his skeleton, teeth and remaining flesh and hair. He was around 6ft tall and had probably been lying underground for around seventy years.

Otherwise, there was nothing else to explain who he was, or how and why he had ended up in an iron coffin. Nothing, that is, until the pathologist started to go through the pockets of the mystery corpse's clothes.

It was the director of the Home Office's Forensic Science Laboratory at Preston, Dr James Brierley Firth, who discovered, amongst other general items on the body, a set of keys, a hallmarked signet ring and two appointment diaries, dating from 1884 and 1885. He also discovered a set of papers, stuck together with the oozing residue of the putrefying cadaver.

With considerable difficulty these were cleaned up, prised apart and spread out, and there were around thirteen sheets in all. These seemed to relate to a Liverpool company called T.C. Williams & Co., of Leeds Street, and one of the papers was a letter addressed to Mr Williams personally. On 19 July 1945 an inquest into the mystery man was opened by the Liverpool coroner but immediately adjourned whilst investigations continued.

Police discovered that such a company had indeed existed in Liverpool at around 1880. This had been a firm of oil traders owned by a Thomas Cregeen Williams, whose home address seemed to have been in the Anfield district of the city. Investigations also revealed that the company had been in severe financial trouble, but no record of the death of Thomas Williams could be found.

This led the police to the inevitable conclusion that the corpse in the iron coffin was Thomas Williams himself. However, this could not be established conclusively, so on 31 August 1945 the coroner closed the inquest by recording an open verdict on 'the death of an unknown man sometime around the summer of 1885'. But the cause of his death could still not be established. As a result, many questions, to this day, remain unanswered:

Was the body that of Thomas Cregeen Williams?

How did he die?

Was it suicide? If so, how did he do it, and who sealed him into his metal tube?

Was it murder? If so, by whom and why was murder committed?

Why such an elaborate coffin?

Why buried so deep and so anonymously, with no marker or record?

And, finally, who dug the hole and put the body in it?

In due course, the remains were cremated and buried in an unmarked plot in a Liverpool cemetery, but what happened to the tube is not recorded. It is unlikely that we shall ever discover the identity or the circumstances surrounding the life and death of the man in the iron coffin.

THE LOST LAKE AND THE GORILLA'S LIPSTICK

Two of Liverpool's most intriguing curiosities are right in the heart of the city, and most people have no idea they exist. One of these is completely hidden, even though it is walked over every day by thousands of people; the other can be seen quite clearly, but you have to know where to look to find it.

West Derby-born architect and sculptor David Backhouse went to Alsop Grammar School in Liverpool and then trained as an architect, qualifying in 1965. He worked for a number of architects firms, but his first independent commission was in 1980, for the Royal Insurance Company, who hired him to build a new shopping and office complex between Harrington Street and Mathew Street in the heart of Liverpool.

The gorilla with the lipstick!
(*Discover Liverpool Library*)

David was considering his design when, on 8 December 1980, John Lennon was shot and killed in New York, by disturbed lone gunman Mark Chapman. This tragedy profoundly affected David, who was very friendly with Cynthia Lennon (*b.*1939), John's first wife, and who knew John too. The following morning David designed the remarkable building that we now know as Cavern Walks, almost as a tribute to the murdered musician.

Work soon began on clearing the site and on excavating the old Cavern Club. This had been closed, and the warehouses above it demolished into the former cellar nightclub, in 1973 when the underground railway Loop Line was being excavated. This was at a time before the city realised what an asset it had as the 'birthplace' of The Beatles.

The local building firm, Tyson's, began the excavations on the site, but as their workmen were digging deep into the ground to build the foundations of the tall building, the ground opened up beneath them to reveal an 8ft-wide shaft, rough-hewn into the sandstone bedrock and sunk to a depth of 40ft. Then they discovered another four shafts, just as wide and all stretching down into the earth. However, and to their great surprise, the shafts all opened onto a massive, apparently natural, subterranean freshwater lake. This was just sitting there in a vast cave – so, yes, there is a cavern beneath the Cavern!

Records were investigated, and what the Victorians had named the Harrington Reservoir was now identified. Filled naturally with fresh water from Liverpool's high water table, Victorian builders had sunk the shafts as wells in the mid-years of the nineteenth century. This was to provide a water supply to all the warehouses and to the new Fruit Exchange Building that were then being built on the ground above.

Overcome by curiosity at the sight of the water glistening mysteriously at the bottom of the shafts, David and some of Tyson's men were lowered down the widest well in a rubber dinghy! Photographs show these intrepid explorers rowing on the lake in stygian darkness, but they did not get far! This was not because the water came to an end, quite the opposite, it seemed to spread out for an uncertain distance and on into a complete unknown!

The pitch black was total, deep below the bustling streets of the city, and the silence was complete, except for the soft lapping of the water against the sides of their tiny craft. This was all so creepy that fear quickly overcame the previously bold architect and his companions, and they quickly paddled back to the bottom of the shaft! Here they were hauled back up to more secure and predictable surroundings.

And the lost lake of Liverpool is still there; sitting in all its ancient mystery under what we now know as Liverpool's Cavern Quarter. David Backhouse's magnificent Cavern Walks opened in 1984, at a cost of £5 million, and it stands suspended over the Harrington Reservoir on great steel girders and a skilfully engineered concrete canopy, all taking the weight of the tall building.

Quite rightly, David was very proud of his work, which is delightfully embellished by terracotta plaques of Tudor Roses and Doves of Peace, all created by Cynthia Lennon. He had successfully designed his new structure to reflect the different styles from all the most significant periods of Liverpool's architectural history. In an interview he gave at the time, David said that it was his belief that buildings should always be designed with people in mind and so 'should be a blend of art and architecture'.

David's comment really upset the renowned architect Norman Foster (b.1935), now 'Sir' Norman. It seems that he regarded the young Liverpudlian architect as an 'upstart'; he pompously dismissed David's opinion by saying that 'art is to architecture like lipstick is to a gorilla' – meaning it is 'completely irrelevant'! Now, we Liverpudlians can throw our toys out of the pram far and hard when upset, but David Backhouse said nothing. In response, he simply put a finishing touch to the exterior of his building.

What David created is the second of the curiosities associated with Cavern Walks, and it can be found high on the outside wall. To see this, visitors make their way along Doran's Lane, off Lord Street, which leads to the entrance to David's shopping, office and apartment complex. However, they do not go inside, they immediately turn left and walk a short way along Harrington Street. Here, and set into the apex of the brick archway that surrounds the large, roller-shutter entrance to the building's underground loading bay, they find the Keystone. This takes the form of another rectangular terracotta panel. However, in the centre of this one can clearly be seen a deeply, and beautifully carved, relief. This shows a gorilla holding a powder-compact and applying lipstick – revenge is a dish best served cold!

The Petrified Forest of Meols

Of the many strange objects that can be found across Merseyside some are either difficult to see or are lost, as are the great fossilised tree-stumps of the north Wirral coast.

The Petrified Forest of Meols. (*Discover Liverpool Library*)

For many years, when there was a particularly low tide between Meols and Moreton dozens of rock-like bases of very ancient trees would be exposed, peeking out above the sands to a height of 1 or 2ft. These are the fossilised remnants of a primeval forest that once covered Merseyside more than 15,000 years ago. As well as the large stumps of these very ancient trees, their great spreading roots would also be revealed, stretching over the sands for up to 6 or 7ft.

Photographs exist of these prehistoric relics, but with the many changes to the coastline that have taken place over the last decades, and because of shifting currents and sandbanks, the last reported sighting was in the spring of 1982 – unless, of course, anyone knows differently!

In fact, Meols is one of the most important archaeological places in the North West and in Britain! It is probable that it was at Meols that the Phoenicians landed when they came to the Wirral and left their strange carvings on the summit of Bidston Hill, over 2½ millennia ago – as we shall discover in my next story. The Romans too, around 2,000 years ago, landed at Meols, when it was already a thriving and important port.

This part of the Wirral coastline was also one of the first places in the North West that the Vikings attacked when they invaded Britain in the tenth century. Relics of these seaborne aggressors can still be found on the Meols and Moreton sands today, and it is said that a Viking longship lies buried under the car park of the Railway Inn in Meols, just along from the local railway station!

The great lost forest remains buried too and is unlikely to ever be seen again. Except, of course, if another of the great storms that so often attack the River Mersey and the coastlines of the Wirral Peninsula shifts the sands once again – we can only hope!

The Pagan Carvings of Bidston Hill and the Cheshire Cat

Bidston Hill on the Wirral and its nearby village have long been the locations for stories of witchcraft and devil worshipping, and locals have passed down these tales and myths for many generations. However, archaeologists and historians now believe that the hill was in use as far back as ancient pagan times as a place of sun worship and human sacrifice, and there are indeed some very strange carvings on its ancient rocks.

No one has been able to date these accurately, but the oldest is probably the 4.5ft-long carving of a sun goddess, which is etched deeply into the flat rock to the north-east of Bidston Observatory. Clearly a female figure, with rays of sunlight coming out of her head, she faces

The Cheshire Cat of *Alice in Wonderland* fame. (*Shutterstock, 75202630*)

the direction of the rising sun on Midsummer's Day. She is thought to have been carved by Norse-Irish invaders some time around AD 1000. Another ancient carving, this one of a horse, can be found on the bare rock north of the observatory, just before the path turns down towards Bidston Village. Other, later rock carvings can be seen on the vertical rock face just south of the observatory.

Many ancient peoples came to prehistoric Britain from all over the world, including the Phoenicians. It is known that they came to Cornwall for tin, and one of their ships has been found as far north as Scotland. This means that it is likely that they came to the Wirral too, possibly around 650 BC, in search of bronze and tin. They would have sailed up the River Dee and the River Mersey before these great waterways had these names. In fact, it is now believed that they might have given the Mersey the name it had when the Romans came here in the first century AD: 'Belisima' – meaning 'bright goddess'.

The figure known as the moon goddess is also carved into the rocks at the top of Bidston Hill and is thought to be the work of the Phoenicians. She has a moon at her feet, which is almost certainly a later, Celtic addition, possibly symbolising the River Mersey. However, her face is cat-like, and the cat goddess was an important deity in the Phoenicians' pantheon of gods and goddesses, who symbolised wealth and success.

If the Phoenicians did leave this image behind when they finally left the Wirral, could their beliefs have been adopted by primitive local people and passed down through their culture and race memories to take on a new significance? The local tribespeople who occupied the Wirral during the time of the Roman invasion were the Carnovii, who were also known as the Cat People because they worshipped these animals, as well as the moon.

Could these be the origins of the mythical Cheshire Cat, which featured in legends well before Lewis Carroll used it in *Alice in Wonderland*? Could the impossibly wide grin on the cat be another race memory of a time of human sacrifice, when throats were cut 'from ear to ear', like a long, gaping grin?

Bidston Hill is certainly the cradle of many such legends and supernatural stories, and many more than there is space to tell in this particular volume of Merseyside Tales!

The Liver Building Birds and Their True Designer

The Three Graces is the relatively new name given to the famous buildings that stand on the Liverpool waterfront, at the Pier Head, and which were all built directly over the former George's Dock. Individually, these are the Port of Liverpool Building, opened in 1907; the Cunard Building, erected in 1916; and the Royal Liver Building, which was opened in 1911. Of the three, this last building is the most iconic and internationally known.

From the top of the Liver Birds that crown each of its two towers, to its base, the building stands at a height of 295ft (90m). This was one of the first multi-storey, reinforced concrete, steel-framed buildings in the world, and its revolutionary design means that its granite exterior is simply cladding. The massive weight of the building is supported on concrete piers that were sunk into the bed of the old George's Dock to a depth of 40ft.

The building was commissioned by the Royal Liver Friendly Society to be their headquarters. This company had adopted the Liver Bird as its emblem because this was the name of the local tavern in which the original society had first met.

The building is crowned by a pair of clock towers. On the east tower, and facing the city, there is one clock face; on the west tower, and over-looking the river, there are clock faces on three sides. This is so that ships on the river can tell the time from any position. Each clock dial is 25ft (7.6m) in diameter, and they are set 220ft above ground. They are each 2½ft wider than those on the Big Ben clock tower in London, and each minute hand is an impressive 14ft long.

Owing to the severity of the weather in the Mersey estuary, each dial has a 3.5-ton iron framework which carries the 660lbs of opal glass necessary to withstand wind pressure of up to 11 tons per square inch. To celebrate their manufacture, one of the clock faces was first used as a unique dining table, with forty guests comfortably seated around the perimeter.

The four dials are driven by a single clock mechanism which is named the Great George. This is because it was started at the precise moment that King George V was crowned, on 22 June 1911. This was accomplished via a telephone link with an observer at Westminster Abbey. The huge timepiece was designed to be accurate to within half a minute a year, and it is the largest electronically driven clock in Britain.

There are no bells serving the Great George clock, but in 1953 electronic chimes were installed to serve as a memorial to the members of the Royal Liver Friendly Society who had died during the two world wars, and these are rung on special occasions in the city.

On top of the dome on each of the clock towers stands a gigantic Liver Bird. These are perhaps the most renowned of all the many hundreds of Liver Birds that are to be found across the city. Said to derive from the cormorants that once nested in the old pool of the town, or from the eagle crest of King John, the bird carries a sprig of seaweed (*lava* in Welsh) in its beak.

The birds on top of the Royal Liver Building are made from hammered copper plates and are bolted together on armatures of rolled steel. They each stand 18ft high, the head of each bird is 3½ft long, each leg has a circumference of 2ft, and the wingspan is 12ft across. The great birds need to be tied down with cables because a legend says that if they ever fly away then Liverpool would be doomed! They are also of different sexes, with the female facing the river. She is waiting for the sailors to return home safely, following their long sea voyages. The male bird stands facing inland. He is watching to see when the pubs have opened!

However, for many years the true designer of these famous sculptures was kept hidden, and most people believe that they were the work of the building's architect, Walter Aubrey Thomas (1859–1934). They are not. They are the creation of Carl Bartels (1866–1955), who was originally denied attribution and credit because he was a German.

Carl Bernard Bartels was a wood carver who had been born in the Black Forest but who had been brought up in Stuttgart. There he had trained under his father, a gifted and recognised wood carver, but in 1887 Carl decided to emigrate to Britain to begin a new life. So at the age of 21 he came here with his young bride, Mathilde Zappe. The couple were very happy in England and both took British nationality. They settled in the London borough of Haringey, where they had a son and a daughter.

The Royal Liver Friendly Society held a competition for the design of the Liver Birds that they wanted to surmount their new building in Liverpool, and Carl wanted to submit a design. But first he had to research his subject, and so he travelled up to Liverpool. In the city's town hall he found a stuffed cormorant and this, together with other images of Liverpool's corporate symbol, formed the basis of his designs.

When he submitted these, both Thomas and the Royal Liver Society were impressed, and Carl was awarded the contract. The two splendid copper birds were then built by the very skilled Bromsgrove Guild, who were part of the Arts and Crafts movement. This had been led by the artist and writer William Morris (1834–1896) and had been influential in British design since 1887.

However, three years after the opening of the Royal Liver Building, the First World War broke out. Now anti-German feeling swept across Britain, and German shops, businesses and homes were attacked, as were many German people. This was especially the case in Liverpool, following the sinking of the passenger liner *Lusitania*, which had been struck by a torpedo fired from a German submarine on 7 May 1915. The Cunarder had been sailing from New York, bound for Liverpool, and she sank with the loss of 1,198 passengers and crew. There were only 761 survivors. In the hysteria following this catastrophe Carl Bartels' blueprints and sketches for the Liver Birds were destroyed. His name was also expunged from the records of the Liver Building's design and construction.

Before this, however, at the outbreak of the war, Carl had already been interned as an enemy alien, even though he had been a naturalised Briton for over twenty years. He was imprisoned, with other German nationals, in a camp on the Isle of Man where conditions were very bad. After the war Carl was forcibly repatriated to Germany and was made to leave his wife and children behind. He was only allowed to return when a sponsor was found who would act as guarantor for him and provide him with work. Back in England, and reunited with his family, Carl continued carving, and he provided a range of designs for Durham Cathedral and a number of stately homes in Britain.

Carl was still denied credit for the creation of the Liver Birds at the Pier Head, and during the Second World War he found work making artificial limbs for wounded servicemen. He died in 1955, with only his family recognising the truth about his singular contribution to Liverpool's cultural and architectural heritage.

However, in the late 1990s the truth was discovered, and in 1998 the Royal Liver Society invited his granddaughter and great-grandchildren to the city as guests of honour. They dined in state in the building their ancestor had so beautifully embellished and were also welcomed by the Lord Mayor.

In 2011, on the 100th anniversary of the Royal Liver Building and at a special ceremony in Liverpool, Tim Olden, the great-grandson of Carl, was awarded the Citizen of Honour Award on behalf of his forbear. I too am delighted to be able to make the work of Carl Bernard Bartels – the true designer of the Royal Liver Building Birds – more widely known and appreciated.

The Devil's Nest at New Brighton

In 1820, on the shore of what is now New Brighton seafront, a short row of huts and shacks had been built to accommodate the men building Fort Perch Rock and the lighthouse. When the work was complete these were abandoned on what was then a largely deserted stretch of coastline. But then, in 1833, a wealthy and successful Liverpool merchant, James Atherton, bought 170 acres of open heathland on the north-east Wirral coast. His plan was to design and build a grand residential town for genteel society, which would attract permanent residents and discerning holiday visitors.

In 1834 he built a wooden ferry pier and began a new ferry service from Liverpool. However, in 1848 the pier was destroyed in a strong gale and had to be rebuilt. As this work was beginning, a single-storey building was quickly erected on the shore near the entrance to the new pier and not far from the row of abandoned shacks. This was made of roughly hewn planks simply nailed or tied together and was owned by a purveyor of all kinds of liquid refreshment, from tea to gin. He had recognised the commercial opportunity of selling to the workmen building the new pier and to anyone else in the vicinity too.

However, by this time Atherton's town was becoming well established. Also, the new residents had aspirations that their new town

The Devil's Nest. (*Courtesy of Liverpool Athenaeum Library*)

should be as cultured as the south coast spa town after which it had been named. They were horrified by the 'liquor shack', and by the fact that it was attracting large numbers of 'unsavoury individuals' to their seaside community, most of whom were drunk, most of the time.

This open invitation to imbibe strong liquor now attracted other entrepreneurs to the previously abandoned huts, which were now soon occupied by 'a coarse community of beach traders and hawkers, and a rowdy element of drunken men and their importuning female companions'. These women were of questionable morals and lewd behaviour, and, as a result, this part of the beachfront became indecent, unsafe and lawless.

Local residents now named this hotbed of vice the Devil's Nest, and day trippers from Liverpool, as well as local people, were increasingly the victims of anti-social behaviour, robbery and drunken assaults. Something had to be done. So in 1874 local people forced the police to take decisive action. They, and the borough authorities, were uncompromising and hired in a large number of temporary 'special constables' to clean up the Devil's Nest. However, and as there were no 'ASBOs' in those days, the men they hired were no better than thugs themselves. The reasoning behind this was that 'fire should be fought with fire' – and so it was.

No quarter was given, and the hawkers, prostitutes, pimps, thieves and ruffians were forcibly evicted and thrown off the sands. Soon the shanty-town community of ramshackle huts, sheds and alcohol stalls were pulled down and the more sedate and refined New Brighton waterfront began to develop. However, the Devil's Nest had certainly left its mark. This was shown by a letter from 'a concerned New Brighton correspondent', which was printed in the *Liverpool Mercury* on 19 September 1876:

> New Brighton – Skeleton Found.
>
> On Tuesday last the workers engaged excavating for the foundation of the New Brighton Aquarium found the skeleton of a human body, which they placed in a shed on the ground. The remains were found about three feet below the flooring of one of the houses that originally stood there, known by the name of the 'Devil's Nest', and which were pulled down two years ago.
>
> Up to this day (Monday) the skeleton still remains in the shed, and, though known to the police, no action has been taken; and my object in writing you is in hope that an inquiry might be held, and so put an end to the indifferent rumour now in circulation, for about eighteen years ago a builder from Seacombe, after leaving here for his home, was never afterwards seen.

As far as I can establish, no such inquiry was ever carried out, nor was the mysterious skeleton ever identified. However, it is likely that this unfortunate soul was a victim of one of the dealers in vice and violence for which New Brighton had previously become notorious.

Nevertheless, and despite this grisly discovery, the Devil's Nest was now nothing more than a bad memory. New Brighton was indeed able to fulfill its ambitions, and it soon became an extremely popular, successful, holiday and seaside resort as well as a settled and quite well-to-do town. It also now provided its visitors with some very special and much more socially acceptable attractions, as we shall see in a later tale.

THE ADMIRAL'S COFFIN

Behind Liverpool Town Hall, on Exchange Flags, stands the Nelson Memorial Statue. This was the first piece of public sculpture ever erected in the city; it was paid for by public subscription and was unveiled in 1813. Liverpool was one of the first towns to commemorate the death of Admiral Horatio Lord Nelson (1758–1805), a great hero to the town. Nelson had kept the oceans clear of Spanish and French warships and privateers, so that the merchant vessels of Liverpool could ply their trade around the seven seas.

Lord Nelson had been killed at the Battle of Trafalgar in 1805, and the memorial is a glorious celebration of the man, and his legend. It comprises a large bronze group, showing, at the top, Nelson being guided from death into eternal life by the goddess Victory, which was, appropriately, the name of the admiral's flagship. The monument also displays four bronze plaques which show scenes from his greatest naval triumphs, at the battles of Cape St Vincent, the Nile at Aboukir Bay, Copenhagen and, of course, Trafalgar.

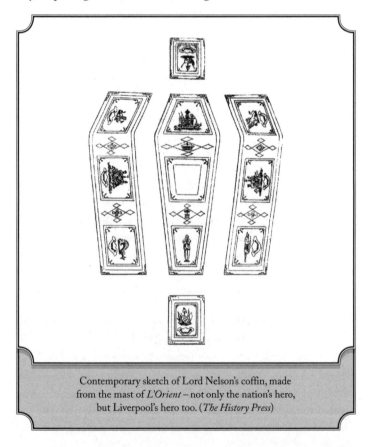

Contemporary sketch of Lord Nelson's coffin, made from the mast of *L'Orient* – not only the nation's hero, but Liverpool's hero too. (*The History Press*)

Around the base of the monument sit the naked male figures of four captives, in chains and racked with anguish. These are not slaves, as is often mistakenly believed, but again representations of the great sailor's naval successes. Circling the statue, and set into its granite base, are the words of Nelson's signal to his fleet at the start of the Battle of Trafalgar: 'England expects that every man shall do his duty.'

And Horatio Nelson certainly did his duty to the nation. During this sea battle the British Navy lost no ships of the line, whilst our enemies – the Spanish and the French – lost all but ten of theirs. The enemy fleets lost 4,408 men, whilst the British lost only 449. But the Memorial Statue is not the only connection that Liverpool has with Nelson.

At Trafalgar he was on the quarterdeck of HMS *Victory* when a French warship sailed to close quarters. A sniper in the enemy ship's top rigging fired a pistol shot that mortally wounded Nelson, who was carried below, where he later died surrounded by his senior officers. Ever a man prepared for any eventuality, Nelson had his own, ready-made coffin on board *Victory*. He had chosen the wood for this whilst fighting at the Battle of Aboukir Bay in 1798. This had been salvaged from the mainmast of the French flagship *L'Orient*, which was a 120-gun warship that had suffered a massive attack by Nelson's fleet and which had burst into flames.

The commander of the French vessel, Captain Casabianca, lay dying on deck and, in all the confusion of falling masts, blazing fires and flying cannonballs, his 12-year-old son, Giocante, refused to leave his father's side. The flames eventually reached the ship's powder magazine and the vessel exploded, killing the boy and cascading wreckage across the battle and the sea. The explosion was heard over 20 miles away, and the great French ship sank with £3 million in Maltese gold still aboard. There was a massive and unintended loss of life, and a stunned silence descended over both fleets at the enormity and the nature of this disaster.

Nelson rescued as many of the survivors as he could and so initiated the code of wartime chivalry at sea.

Felicia Hemans (1793–1835) was a famous Victorian poetess who was born at No. 118 Duke Street in Liverpool and who later moved to No. 7 High Street in Wavertree. She wrote plays, hymns, song lyrics and anthologies of verse, but perhaps her most famous poem is 'Casabianca'. This was published in 1826 and tells the tale of the loss of *L'Orient*, celebrating the sacrifice and love that young Giocante Casabianca had for his stricken father:

The boy stood on the burning deck, whence all but he had fled,
The flame that lit the battles wreck, shone round him o'er the dead.
Yet, beautiful and bright he stood, As born to rule the storm;
A creature of heroic blood, A proud, though child-like form.
The flames rolled on—he would not go, without his Father's word;
That father, faint in death below, His voice no longer heard.
He called aloud—'say, Father, say if yet my task is done?'
He knew not that the chieftain lay, Unconscious of his son.

The Nelson Memorial in Exchange Flags, Liverpool.
(*Discover Liverpool Library*)

After Trafalgar, Nelson's body was shipped back to Britain in a barrel of brandy, to preserve it, but when it was opened all the alcohol had gone! This had not evaporated. During the voyage sailors on board had been taking draughts of brandy from the cask in order to take into themselves something of their great admiral's courage and heroism; taking a tot of brandy whilst at sea has been known as 'tapping the admiral' ever since!

Lord Nelson now lies inside the coffin, made from the mast of *L'Orient*, in a great tomb in the crypt of St Paul's Cathedral in London – not only the nation's hero but Liverpool's hero too.

St Patrick's Cross – Over 1,000 Years of Pilgrimage

There are many sites of Christian pilgrimage throughout Europe but few can be older than Saint Patrick's Cross in Liverpool. Located now in a tiny and obscure cul-de-sac known as Standish Street, which sits off Crosshall Street in the city centre, can be found a small, beautifully maintained garden. It is here, many people believe, that in AD 432, and on the instructions of Pope Celestine, St Patrick preached his final sermon before setting sail on a treacherous voyage to Ireland, to convert the people there to Christianity.

Patrick was born in Roman-occupied Britain, although the precise location is uncertain, as is the year of his birth, although this is generally accepted to have been sometime between the years 376 and 405. Venerated for many centuries, especially by Irish Roman Catholics, there are many legends associated with this popular saint. These include the story that he banished all the snakes from Ireland, driving them into the sea, and that he used the three leaves of the shamrock to explain the Holy Trinity.

Saint Patrick.
(*LOC, LC-USZ62-31937*)

In his own writings Patrick describes how, at the age of 16, he had been captured from his home by pirates and sold into slavery in Ireland. Trapped there for six years, he worked as a shepherd and developed a strong Christian faith. However, one night whilst he was asleep, an angel visited him in a dream and told him how to escape. When he awoke he followed the angel's instructions precisely and indeed found his way home to Britain.

Wanting to learn more about Christianity, he travelled to Gaul (modern France), where he studied under Saint Germain, who was Bishop of Auxerre. Twelve years later he returned to Britain. There he felt a calling to return as a missionary to Ireland, and the Pope confirmed this. It was then that he was sent back to Ireland on a mission that was to last for thirty years.

It is thought that Saint Patrick died between 460 and 493, and he is said to be buried in the cathedral in Downpatrick, in County Down in Northern Ireland. His annual feast day is boisterously celebrated around the world, especially in Liverpool, on 17 March.

For centuries before the Reformation, and for centuries afterwards, although then in great secrecy, Christians from all over Britain and abroad would come to the obscure site outside what was to eventually become the town of Liverpool. Here they would worship around a commemorative cross that had been erected to the saint. Although there are no records stating when the monument first appeared, presumably it was a stone cross, perhaps set on steps or a pedestal.

Around the cross these pilgrims would give thanks for Patrick's life and work, and pray for themselves and others. Until the nineteenth century this part of Liverpool remained outside the town boundary, in what was still a rural part of the surrounding countryside. Nevertheless, the position of the cross appears on the earliest maps, showing that it was a significant local feature.

But during the Puritan era of the seventeenth century and the Jacobite Rebellions of the eighteenth century, people found worshipping at such an obviously Catholic site would have been severely punished. In fact, it was only after the final routing of the Scottish Catholic Rebels in 1745 that hostility towards Catholics began to relax somewhat. Although damaged, a portion of the cross seems to have survived through these turbulent times. There are reports of it as late as 1775, but soon after this the cross disappeared, although its original location remained a site of pilgrimage.

In 1791, the passing of the Roman Catholic Relief Act allowed Catholics to worship openly once again, provided that their chapels were registered with the authorities. Eventually, and with the subsequent passing of the Catholic Emancipation Act in 1829, Catholics were also finally allowed to vote and sit in Parliament.

It was after this that Catholicism began to become accepted again, and the local population of Catholics was suddenly swelled to very large numbers, with the influx of hundreds of thousands of desperate, starving people into Liverpool, fleeing from the Irish Potato Famine of the 1840s.

It was then that the site of Saint Patrick's Cross, in its previously out-of-the way backwater, became a centre of settlement for these Irish Catholics. Knowing of this holy place dedicated to their patron saint, thousands of them moved into the area. Soon streets of terraced and back-to-back houses covered the once rural landscape. The location of Saint Patrick's Cross now became the focal point of this new community, and in 1860 a church was built over the site. This was Holy Cross church, and its altar was placed directly over the sacred spot.

The new church served the large Catholic community, which was made up not only of Irish people but also of a significant number of Italian families that had settled in the district. These people created a part of Liverpool that became known as 'Little Italy'.

The church was destroyed by a Nazi incendiary bomb in 1941 but was completely rebuilt in 1954. However, with the decline of Liverpool during the 1970s and 1980s the population of the area rapidly reduced. So much so that the Roman Catholic Archdiocese could no longer justify keeping Holy Cross church open, and in 2004, and in the face of much local opposition, the church was demolished.

Nevertheless, members of the congregation and other people from the remaining community were determined not to let the significance of the location, or of their local parish, vanish under the bulldozers that were now knocking down their streets and homes. As the once-long streets were replaced with the tiny cul-de-sac of Standish Street, with its dozen or so attractive bungalows, these people decided to recreate the site of pilgrimage.

This is why there is a small, well-kept area of lawn and flowerbeds, surrounded by low railings and shaded by trees, in the centre of this secluded and now little-known close. Here, as well as some memorial plaques and tablets, is a large sandstone cross that originally stood inside Holy Cross church. The tiny garden is also home to part of the foundation stone and stained glass from the church. As well as this, two time capsules are buried in the ground, containing other artefacts from this once-important parish and its congregation.

However, the most powerful object to be seen in this very special memorial garden is contained within a large, transparent, vandal-proof display-case. This stands against a tall brick wall on one side of Standish Street. Inside this is a beautifully painted, lovingly carved, life-size pietá, which is the name given to a statue of the Virgin Mary cradling in her lap the crucified body of her son, Jesus Christ – *pietá* translates as 'pity'.

Whether you have a faith or not, and whether or not that faith is Christianity, I suggest that most people would be moved by this celebration of community and of religious belief, as well as by the silent tranquillity of the garden, hidden away as it is from the noise and traffic of Liverpool's busy city-centre roads.

THE ROBIN HOOD STONE

On Booker Avenue in Liverpool, at its junction with the appropriately named Archerfield Road, stands one of the city's ancient relics: the Robin Hood Stone.

Surrounded by protective iron railings, this is an 8ft high, 3.5ft wide sandstone monolith, deeply scored from centuries of what is presumed to be arrow-sharpening. Before being resited, in August 1928, the stone stood in a nearby field known as Stone Hey, but it was moved when its original location was being built over by the houses that now cover the area. A plaque on the base of the stone records this.

Whilst it is known that local archers lived and worked here in medieval times, in the service of the local landowner Sir Richard Molyneux, there is, of course, no basis to the legend that claims that Robin Hood once stayed in the district and sharpened his arrows on the stone. However, the stone is of considerable archaeological and historical significance.

During the Hundred Years War, which was fought between the English and the French in the fourteenth and fifteenth centuries, all able-bodied English men, and boys over the age of 12, no matter in what part of the country they lived, by law had to be proficient at the longbow. They would practise, and keep their arrows sharp, in case the lord of the manor or the king summoned an army to go to battle.

Local archers sharpened their arrows on the Robin Hood Stone, and finding objects like this all over England is not so exceptional.

The reputation for the deadly precision and fearlessness of the English archers was legendary amongst our enemies. This became particularly true following the Battle of Crecy in 1346 and of Agincourt in 1415. A bowman could release ten arrows a minute, so that by the time the first one had landed another one would be in flight. They were not just fast: English archers were deadly accurate and their bows were extremely powerful. This meant that a skilled man – and all those called to military service had to be – could put an arrow through an enemy's helmet visor at 200yds.

A fifteenth-century archer. Men like this one wore grooves into the Robin Hood Stone by sharpening their arrows. (*The History Press*)

So if our men were ambushed or captured in battle and were not slain, the first two fingers of their right hands would be chopped off so that they could no longer draw their longbows. They would then be sent back to their own lines as a warning to the English. However, this only provoked the archers to greater ferocity against the French.

Also, and as a result of this particular French reprisal, as the English archers lined up on the battlefield in front of the opposing force, prior to an attack, they would brandish their two bow-drawing fingers at the enemy. This demonstration of bravado would also act as a threat and a warning. This has given rise to the unproven belief that this is how the raising of two fingers, as a gesture of abuse and aggression, passed into the British lexicon of 'non-verbal communication'!

Mouse Pie and a Touch of Toad

All over Cheshire and Lancashire during the eighteenth and nineteenth centuries many folk remedies and medicines were in common use. One that was very popular in rural communities, and which was brought into rapidly growing Liverpool, was a cure for children who wet the bed – mouse pie! The recipe consisted of catching and killing mice and baking them into pastry.

The common toad; an ancient miracle cure?
(*Shutterstock, 89992081*)

Alternatively, the tiny rodents could be dried out so that they were completely desiccated; then the fur, flesh and bones would be ground into a powder. This could then either be baked into a pie or, indeed, mixed with milk or water and drunk three times a day!

Mouse pies were baked by caring mothers who would then feed them to their children, and this was believed to be very effective! In fact, it had been a traditional remedy for centuries. Indeed, Dr Barnardo, who was born in 1845 and founded orphanages and a national charity that still bears his name, recommended mouse pie enthusiastically! However, it seems that the mere threat of being fed a mouse pie was enough to cure most children of their bed-wetting – it would work for me!

If you were simply feeling out of sorts during the early decades of the nineteenth century then you might try a drink of Dog's Nose. This is mentioned by Charles Dickens in *The Pickwick Papers*. Recipes varied, but it could be a mixture of beer and gin or of ale and rum. It could also be made by mixing warm porter with moist sugar, gin and nutmeg. If this didn't perk you up, you could always wait for the itinerant Toad Doctor, who particularly frequented Cheshire and the Wirral around this time, to come around to your village.

This eccentric medic would cut off the hind legs of toads brought to him by his patients, and then put them into small bags, which he hung round the neck of those who suffered from 'King's Evil', otherwise known as scrofula. This was also supposed to cure other swellings, rashes or diseases of the skin, and the bags would then be worn against the affected area until the legs inside were entirely rotted. The doctor travelled around in his own pony and trap, and charged 7s for each treatment, which was at least an entire week's wages for many of his patients.

Other remedies offered by the Toad Doctor included wrapping the right foot of a frog in a deer's skin and keeping it about your person to prevent gout. Or you could always cure sore eyes by catching a live frog and licking its eyes. Then you held the frog against your own afflicted eye in the hope that the frog would lick you back – and your cure would be instantaneous! Makes you feel happier about the NHS now, doesn't it?

New Brighton Tower and Pleasure Gardens

With the removal of the Devil's Nest, and with serious investment by the local Wallasey Corporation as well as by private entrepreneurs, the seaside resort of New Brighton went from strength to strength. All kinds of attractions were now appearing to tempt the many thousands of trippers who were now regularly coming to the resort aboard the ferry from Liverpool. They were also coming here from across the Wirral and from further afield too, which prompted, in 1896, the formation of the New Brighton Tower Company. In this new company's share prospectus their stated aim was for the 'construction of an iron tower to rival the Eiffel Tower in Paris'. This tower would rise from spectacular new Tower Building and be surrounded by the Tower Pleasure Grounds, all of which would contain a wealth of attractions and activities.

The New Brighton Tower opened in 1900, at a cost of £120,000, and it had been deliberately built to stand at 567ft high. This was almost 50ft higher above sea level than the Blackpool Tower, which was only 518ft high. The new tower had been designed to attract holidaymakers from the mill towns of Lancashire and the Midlands, away from other resorts like Blackpool and Morecambe, and it was the tallest structure in the country at the time. It had four lifts to carry

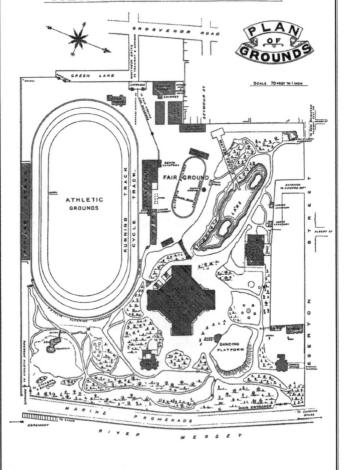

Plan of the Tower Pleasure Grounds at New Brighton.
(*Courtesy of Liverpool Athenaeum Library*)

people right up to the top, from where the views were truly spectacular, and the fare for this was only 6*d*.

The tower stood in 35 acres of grounds, which had already opened on Whit Monday in 1897. Here, in the grounds excited and enthralled visitors would find beautiful gardens and delightful woodlands to stroll though, a Japanese cafe and a boating lake that had gondolas for hire, poled by singing gondoliers! There was a fairground with all the latest mechanical rides, including the thrilling Water Shute. There was even a scenic 'Himalayan' railway that wound its way around the lake, and there was music and entertainment at every turn.

At night the grounds were illuminated by 30,000 red, green and white fairy lights, which looked dazzling to the people walking around the grounds but especially enticing and magical to people looking across at them from the Liverpool side of the river.

The Tower Company also built an athletic arena in their grounds where a variety of sporting events were held. They also staged spectacular shows here including, throughout the summer of 1908, a 'Wild West and Indian Congress'. This included cowboys defending their stagecoach from an Indian attack, bucking broncos, sharp-shooting and steer-herding. However, new regulations prevented American cattle being brought into the country, so wild highland cattle from Scotland had to be used instead! The perimeter of the athletics ground formed a racetrack and speedway that was home to cycle, and later motorcycle, racing.

The tower rose from the centre of the magnificent Tower Building, which contained ballrooms, cafes, restaurants, bars and exhibition halls. It had its own huge theatre, the stage of which was large enough to take a complete circus. This was home to some spectacular productions and to performances by some of the world's greatest entertainers. These included Sir Harry Lauder, Dame Clara Butt, Vesta Tilley and Mae West. The Tower Ballroom even had its own symphony orchestra, which was ranked as one of the finest in the country. In 1898 Sir Edward Elgar conducted a performance of his own *Enigma Variations* here.

There was a monkey house and an aviary, and even a shooting gallery. In 1902 the *Wallasey District Guide* described the Tower Building in the following terms:

The theatre can accommodate 3,500 people, and has the largest stage of any theatre in the kingdom, excepting Drury Garden. Two performances are given daily during the season, and the best known variety artists are engaged, and on Sundays classical concerts are held in the ballroom; most of the leading vocalists of the day are included in the programme, and the orchestra numbers close on 100, the programmes comprising the works of the most celebrated of the past and present.

A Café-Chantant, conducted on Parisian lines, open free to visitors, is a popular feature, performances being given daily at 3pm and 8pm, no charge whatsoever being made for admission. The ballroom, with inlaid parquetry floor, built on 2,000 carriage springs, makes of the finest dancing floors in the country. The menagerie contains a fine collection of animals, including two of the handsomest lions in Europe. The cycle track is pronounced by many professionals the best and fastest in the world.

Two billiards saloons, containing eight tables made by Ashcroft, have been recently added.

After the First World War, due to a lack of regular maintenance, the New Brighton Tower had begun to decay and indeed had been allowed to rot. In 1918 it was declared unsafe and closed down. Money was not available to repair it and, understandably, the local council did not want to foot the bill. There was no alternative and so, between 1919 and 1921, the great New Brighton Tower was taken down.

Tower Buildings remained, however, but still known simply as 'The Tower', and it continued to provide dance hall and other entertainment facilities well into the 1960s. The grand ballroom played host to some of the most popular dance bands of the 1930s and 1940s, and then to skiffle and rock groups in the 1950s.

The Beatles, in the 1960s, made twenty-seven appearances at 'The Tower', as did many other national and international stars, such as Joe Brown, the Rolling Stones and Little Richard. The Beatles made their final appearance at New Brighton Tower on 14 June 1963, topping a bill that included Gerry and the Pacemakers.

Many young couples over the decades did their courting in New Brighton Tower Building, and many marriages and families owe their existence to this very special entertainment venue! But on 5 April 1969 a disastrous fire swept through the structure and completely gutted it.

The blaze could be seen across the river in Liverpool and many people, including myself, saw their happy memories being consumed by the fire. It was a sad day indeed when the building was demolished soon afterwards.

By the end of the 1970s the last remnants of the fairground, which had survived the fire, had been closed and swept away. All that now remains of New Brighton Tower, Tower Building and the Tower Pleasure Grounds is an area of grassed parkland. However, New Brighton itself is currently experiencing a major social, economic and environmental revival, and it is once again an attractive and growing seaside resort.

THE CHILDE OF HALE – THE GENTLE GIANT

In my earlier stories about the township of Hale I made reference to the local 'giant', and it was here, in 1578, that John Middleton was born. He grew up and lived in a small, thatched, whitewashed cottage that still stands today almost unaltered, at least on the outside.

The remarkable thing about John was that by age of 20 he had grown to a height of 9ft 3in, and he had been named locally as 'The Childe of Hale'. This was not an ironic reference to his height but a genuinely affectionate term because of his simple nature and kindly personality. Soon 'The Childe of Hale' became well known far outside his home village, and he was renowned throughout England as being the 'tallest man in the world'!

Inside his cottage, with its low roof, the ceiling had to be removed so that he could stand upright, and his hat pegs were set at 10ft above the floor. Even so, the front and back doors remained a normal size, so John must have had to bend almost double to get in and out of his home!

Sir Gilbert Ireland (c.1559–1626) was Lord of the Manor of Hale at this time, and in 1604, because of John's renown, he decided to employ the gentle giant as his personal bodyguard, 'to walk with him; to stand behind his chair at meals; and to perform feats of strength for his friends'. However, this was more to add to his status as a minor aristocrat rather than for any practical purpose, although John was certainly powerfully built and very strong.

The modern, life-size bronze statue of John Middleton
stands in front of Hale Manor House.
(*Discover Liverpool Library*)

The reputation of the 'Childe of Hale' had now spread so far that
it had reached the ears of King James I in London. Wanting to see
for himself if the stories were true, in 1617 the monarch invited
Sir Gilbert and his gigantic manservant to come to the capital. Here,
said the king, he would set John to fight his own Royal Champion,
who was described as being 'a huge wrestler of prodigious proportions'!

Even though by this time John was now almost 40 years of age,
he and Sir Gilbert made the long and arduous journey to London,
going most of the way on foot! Before setting off, however, and as
they were going to London to see the king, Sir Gilbert presented John
with a beautiful and colourful suit of new clothes for the trip. This was
the talk of Hale and, in due course, of London and the Royal Court!
A description of the outfit, written at the time, said:

They dizened him off with large lace ruffs about his neck and hands;

a striped doublet of crimson and white around his waist;

a blue girdle embroidered with gold;

large white plush breeches, powdered with blue flowers;

green stockings;

broad shoes of a light colour, having high red heels and tied with bows
of red ribbon;

and just below his knees were bandages of the same colour, with large bows.

By his side, a sword was suspended by a broad belt over his shoulder,
and embroidered as his girdle, with blue and gold, and with the
addition of a gold fringe upon the edge.

This must have been a spectacular suit indeed, especially for such a large and otherwise ordinary man. Nevertheless, there is every reason to assume that John was very proud of his appearance, as was Sir Gilbert. A life-size portrait of John, in his 'London' clothes and painted at the time, still hangs in Speke Hall, close to John's home village.

The wrestling match for the king was 'no-contest', with John Middleton winning the bout by a throw and snapping the thumb of James's champion in the process. John's prize was a 20-guinea purse, even though the result infuriated the king and his courtiers because most of them had bet heavily against the 'peasant from the North'! Because of this, John and Sir Gilbert were made to feel very unwelcome and were encouraged to leave London right away. And so the two men began to make their way home but via Brasenose College in Oxford, where Sir Gilbert had been a student. Sir Gilbert stayed on here for some time, meeting up with old friends, and John was the toast of the university city.

However, John only stayed a few days and soon left to continue his journey on his own and, just outside Oxford, he fell in with some fellow travellers. Sadly, these men were not the new friends that naïve and simple John had taken them to be. His new companions understood only too well who John was, and how much money he was carrying. They were footpads and, no matter how big he was, the kindly man was outnumbered and out-matched by this gang of thugs.

At an isolated spot on the long trek home they set upon him, beat him severely, stole his clothes to leave him virtually naked, and robbed him of his prize-purse. Injured and humiliated, John had to complete his journey in pain and completely alone.

Even though he arrived back to a very warm welcome and the love and care of his own community at Hale, John was now a much poorer man than when he had set off. This was especially the case because his stolen prize money was to have been his pension.

Nevertheless, the 'Childe of Hale' was cherished by his fellow villagers, particularly the children, and his simple manner and childlike ways ensured that he was never lonely or short of friendship, even though he never married or had children of his own. However, John Middleton received no compensation from Sir Gilbert when the lord of the manor returned home himself. He simply allowed John to continue to work for him, but only as a field hand. In fact, in the records of the time it was reported that John 'was oblig'd to follow the plow to his dying day'. The work must have been very hard, even for someone as strong as John, or perhaps his severe beating had weakened him, because six years later, in 1623, John died at the age of only 45.

The gentle 'Childe of Hale' now lies in the burial ground of his village church of St Mary. His grave is surrounded by railings, marking out John Middleton, quite rightly, as someone very special indeed.

Select Bibliography

As well as sourcing information from a very wide range of articles, pamphlets, newspapers, periodicals, reports, and official documents, and from many conversations and interviews with some extremely knowledgeable and enthusiastic individuals, my principal sources include:

Around Wallasey and New Brighton by Ralph Rimmer

Birkenhead Priory: A Closer Look by Caroline Croasdale

Buildings of Liverpool, by various

The Changing Face of Liverpool: 1207–1727 by Gill Chitty

Chinese Liverpudlians by Maria Lin Wong

The Churches of Liverpool by David Lewis

Classical Liverpool by Hugh Hollinghurst

Discovering Historic Wavertree by Mike Chitty

The Gangs of Liverpool by Michael Macilwee

Great Liverpudlians by David Charters

Guide to Liverpool 1902 by various

Herdman's Liverpool by William Jackson

The Hidden Places of Lancashire and Cheshire by Jo Noel-Stevens & Martin Stevens

The History of Hale by Peter Hatton

The Hitlers of Liverpool by Michael Unger

John Foster and Sons – Kings of Georgian Liverpool by Hugh Hollinghurst

Liverpolitania by Peter Howell Williams

Liverpool City of Architecture by Quentin Hughes

Liverpool Firsts by Jack Cooper

Liverpool History Society Journal 2002 by various

Liverpool in the Sixteenth Century by Janet Hollinshead

Liverpool Town Books 1649–1671 edited by Michael Power

Liverpool by George Chandler

Liverpool, Birkenhead and New Brighton by various

Lost Villages of Liverpool: Parts 1, 2 and 3 by Derek Whale

Maritime Mercantile City by John Hinchliffe

Memories of Old Liverpool and Its People by Councillor Anthony McVeigh

Mersey Stars: An A-Z of Entertainers by Michael Smout

The Mersey Tunnel by various

Mitres and Missions in Lancashire by Peter Doyle

Old Lancashire Tales by Frank Hird

Old Merseyside Tales by Frank Hird

Olde Liverpoole and Its Charter by Charles Hand

A Passion For Natural History by Clemency Fisher

Public Sculpture of Liverpool by Terry Cavanagh

Romance of Ancient Liverpool by Joseph P. Pearce

The Story of Liverpool by F.A. Bailey and R. Millington

The Streets of Liverpool by James Stonehouse

Underground Liverpool by Jim Moore

Well I Never Noticed That: Parts 1 & 2 by Andrew F. Richardson

Wirral Smugglers, Wreckers, and Pirates by Gavin Chappell

ABOUT THE AUTHOR

Born and bred in Liverpool, Ken Pye is the managing director of The Knowledge and is in demand across Britain and Europe as a business-development mentor, programme and conference facilitator, and as a motivational speaker at major conferences and business events. Ken is also a Fellow at Liverpool Hope University, a Fellow of the Royal Society of Arts, and a Proprietor of the Liverpool Athenaeum.

In a varied career spanning over forty years, Ken has experience in all professional sectors. This includes working with profoundly disabled youngsters as a youth and community leader, as the community development worker for Toxteth, the North West Regional Officer for Barnardos, the National Partnership Director for the Business Environment Association and as Senior Programme Director with Common Purpose.

In addition, Ken is the managing director of Discover Liverpool, and as such is a recognised expert on the past, present and future of his home city and region. He is a frequent contributor to journals, magazines and newspapers, and is a popular after-dinner speaker. He is also a regular broadcaster for both radio and television.

Ken is the author of the acclaimed books *Discover Liverpool* and *The Bloody History of Liverpool*, as well as a principal contributor to the popular *Scousers* and the author of *A Brighter Hope*, about the founding and history of Liverpool Hope University, which is published by Liverpool Hope University Press.

Having also completed two private writing commissions for the Earl of Derby, Ken has also recently published *Liverpool: The Rise, Fall, and Renaissance of a World Class City* and *Liverpool Pubs*.

Ken is also the writer and presenter of the series of *Discover Liverpool* DVDs, the third edition of which has recently been issued.

If you have enjoyed this book you might also enjoy Ken's audio CD series, entitled *Curious Characters and Tales of Merseyside*, which are readily available.

On a personal basis, and if pressed (better still, if taken out to dinner), Ken will regale you with tales about his experiences during the Toxteth Riots, as a bingo caller, as the lead singer of a pop group and as a mortuary attendant.

Ken is married to Jackie and they have three children: Ben, Samantha, and Danny.

Visit Ken's website at www.discover-liverpool.com

Also from The History Press

MERSEYSIDE

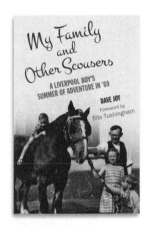

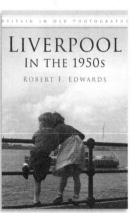

Find these titles and more at
www.thehistorypress.co.uk

Also from The History Press

BLOODY BRITISH HISTORY

Britain has centuries of incredible history to draw on – everything from Boudica and the Black Death to the Blitz. This local series, harking back to the extraordinary pulp magazines of days gone by, contains only the darkest and most dreadful events in your area's history. So embrace the nastier side of British history with these tales of riots and executions, battles and sieges, murders and regicides, witches and ghosts, death, devilry and destruction!

Also from The History Press

We are proud to present our historical crime fiction imprint, The Mystery Press, featuring a dynamic and growing list of titles written by diverse and respected authors, united by the distinctiveness and excellence of their writing. From a collection of thrilling tales by the CWA Short Story Dagger award-winning Murder Squad, to a Victorian lady detective determined to solve some sinister cases of murder in London, these books will appeal to serious crime fiction enthusiasts as well as those who simply fancy a rousing read.

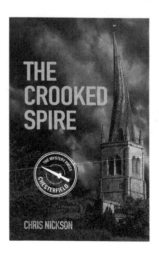

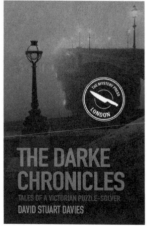

Also from The History Press

BACK TO SCHOOL